# HOW TO FIND
# YOUR FAMILY HISTORY
# IN U.S. CHURCH RECORDS:
## A GENEALOGIST'S GUIDE

Sunny Jane Morton and
Harold A. Henderson, CG

Genealogical Publishing Co., Inc.

Published by Genealogical Publishing Company, 2019
Baltimore, Maryland

Library of Congress Control Number 2019940012

ISBN 9780806320953

*Made in the United States of America*

*To all those who wrote and kept
church record books
through many long centuries,
even those who didn't write
as much as we wished.*

# CONTENTS

# INTRODUCTION

This book will help genealogists and other historical researchers tackle a surprisingly neglected resource: records created by the major Christian denominations before 1900 in the United States.

Many U.S. churches documented their members' lives long before governments did. Even when civil records do exist, the corresponding religious records may reveal unique details. Furthermore, church registers may identify those who go unnamed in other records: women, children, ethnic minorities, immigrants, and the poor. We often find ancestors' births, maiden or married names, marriage details, deaths, family relationships, other residences, and even immigrants' overseas birthplaces noted in the records. And because church records weren't kept at courthouses, they often survived disasters that destroyed other local records.

Though church records aren't available for every ancestor, there's never been a better time to make them a routine part of the research process. Online tools can help you identify possible ancestral churches and track down surviving records. Records that once took years to find and visit are now within much easier reach, including millions that have been digitized and indexed online.

That's where this unique book comes in. *How to Find Your Family History in U.S. Church Records* takes readers step-by-step through the process of identifying, locating, and gaining access to these genealogical gems; included are hundreds of links to church records and to the resources that will help readers find them. Online resources are proliferating but church records don't always reveal themselves: effort and expertise are often required to find relevant records. This peer-reviewed book offers a reader-friendly but solid methodological approach, with practical strategies and examples on such all-important topics as these:

- What may be in church records that make them worth pursuing.
- How to determine which church an ancestor belonged to—or at least make an educated guess.
- How to trace a church's affiliation and record-keeping practices to the present day.
- How to access records, even if the church itself has disappeared.
- Major U.S. church record collections that are available online.
- Must-know information for several of the larger and more influential denominations: historical background, governance, terminology, record types and content, affiliated churches, and information about church archives and libraries. More than thirty archivists, historians, and genealogical experts in specific faith traditions have contributed their knowledge to these denominational chapters!

To include all faiths and carry them through the 20th century would have doubled the size of the book and postponed its completion indefinitely. Recognizing that perfection is the enemy of completion, we encourage others to extend and improve upon this work. Many important faiths that have grown up in the U.S. or been brought here by immigrants are not represented in this book; their stories and records deserve to be respected, described, explained, and cataloged as well. We would especially love to see more updated inventories and descriptions of the extant records of historically African American churches.

We gratefully acknowledge the following experts who have generously shared their knowledge and encouragement, though any errors or omissions are our fault, not theirs. We also apologize if any have inadvertently been overlooked in this list:

- Suzanne Russo Adams, AG, FamilySearch Senior Content Strategist, Southern European genealogy expert
- Lisa Parry Arnold, author of *Thee and Me: A Beginner's Guide to Early Quaker Records*
- John D. Beatty, CG, Volunteer Archivist, Episcopal Diocese of Northern Indiana
- James M. Beidler, German genealogy expert
- Richard Berg, Evangelical and Reformed Church archivist emeritus
- Jay G. Burrup, Church History Specialist/Archivist, Church History Library, The Church of Jesus Christ of Latter-day Saints
- James Cooper, Congregational Library, Director, "New England's Hidden Histories"
- Caryn M. Dalton, MARE, MASM, Reference Assistant, United Theological Seminary, Dayton, Ohio
- David B. Eller, Editor, *Brethren Roots*
- J. Eric Elliott, Archivist, Moravian Archives
- Russell L. Gasero, Archivist, The Archives of the Reformed Church in America
- Phil Haas, Director of Archives, Catholic Diocese of Cleveland
- Jane Higle, Archivist, The Wesleyan Church
- Carol Holliger, Archivist, Archives of Ohio United Methodism
- Loren L. Johns, Ph.D., Professor of New Testament, Anabaptist Mennonite Biblical Seminary
- Karen Mauer Jones, CG, FGBS, New York and Dutch colonial/Huguenot genealogy expert
- William Kostlevy, Director, Brethren Historical Library and Archives
- Dr. Michael D. Lacopo, German/Swiss genealogy expert
- Peggy Clemens Lauritzen, AG, FOGS, Southern/Appalachian genealogy expert
- Laura Mars, Reference Manager, Concordia Historical Institute (Lutheran)
- Roger P. Minert, Ph.D., AG, Professor of Family History, Brigham Young University
- Bryan L. Mulcahy, Reference Librarian, Fort Myers Regional Library, Florida, WPA records expert
- Randy L. Neuman, Associate Director of Library Services, Director, United Brethren Historical Center, Huntington University
- Dana Ann Palmer, CG, Midwestern research expert
- Dr. Paul Peucker, Archivist of the Moravian Church in America, Northern Province; Editor, *Journal of Moravian History*
- Tim Pinnick, African American history and records expert
- Elissa Scalise Powell, CG, CGL, Pennsylvania and Moravian records expert
- Virginia F. Rainey, Stated Clerk, Presbytery of Huntingdon, Presbyterian historian
- Hunt Schenkel, Archivist, Schwenkfelder Library & Heritage Center, Pennsburg, Pennsylvania
- Kip Sperry, Professor of Church History and Doctrine, Brigham Young University; author, *A Guide to Mormon Family History Sources*

- Joe Springer, Curator, Mennonite Historical Library, Goshen College, Goshen, Indiana
- Bill Sumners, CA, Director, Southern Baptist Historical Library and Archive
- John D. Thiesen, Archivist, Co-director of Libraries, Mennonite Library and Archives, Bethel College, North Newton, Kansas
- Gwen Gosney Erickson, Librarian and Archivist, Quaker Archives, Guilford College

In addition, Sunny Morton thanks her husband, Jeremy Morton, for his enduring and selfless support. She thanks other influential cheerleaders: her parents, Richard and Cheryl McClellan; her aunt Judie Greenhalgh; Anne Sindelar and the Genealogical Committee of the Western Reserve Historical Society; Deborah Abbott, Ph.D.; Lisa Louise Cooke; George G. Morgan; Jim Beidler; and the readers and class attendees who kept requesting this book.

# PART 1

# *Family History Research in Church Records*

## *Chapter 1*

# WHAT'S IN CHURCH RECORDS?

Not all of our ancestors were religious, and those who were religious did not all affiliate with a church. But many did so, and that relationship—whether tenuous or devoted—may have generated records from birth to burial and several stops in between.

For centuries church records were inscribed in blank books, where clerks or clergy created handwritten columns or simply wrote entries in individual, unformatted rows. Preprinted registers came into use in the late 1800s. Either way, the records may tell of births, deaths, relatives, baptisms, ethnicity, national origin, confirmations, marriages, memberships, dismissals, migrations, ministries, and personal beliefs.

## WHAT YOU MAY LEARN FROM CHURCH RECORDS

### Births

Few churches kept separate lists of births for children of adult members. Usually birth information is embedded in infant baptismal records (and, with low frequency, in adult baptismal records). Even when a baby was baptized some months after birth, the record is still important, given that information recorded at or near the time of an event is more likely to be accurate. Other things being equal, birth information in a baptismal record is generally more reliable than birth information that appears later.

### Relatives' names

Relatives and potential relatives often appear in church records, which may also specify family relationships, particularly those of parents and spouses. Parents' names may appear in infant baptismal records, lists of births to church members, and occasionally in marriage records (most commonly for Quakers). Some churches created family records showing the names of parents and all their children. In other cases, you may be able to reconstruct a family group from various entries made over the course of several years, such as the marriage record of a couple and the subsequent baptisms of children born to that couple, especially if witnesses or godparents were recorded.

### National origin or ethnicity

Affiliation with a particular church may suggest an ancestor's national origin or ethnicity. Some congregations—e.g., Dutch Reformed, German Lutheran, African Methodist Episcopal, and Anglican (Church of England)—served particular groups. In the late 1800s and early 1900s, hundreds of Catholic national parishes were organized to serve German, Irish, Slovakian, and other immigrant communities.

Church records may provide more specific information about members' geographic origins as well. One study found that German-American church records reveal immigrants' overseas hometowns about 65–75 percent of the time, more than three times as often as the next-best sources: military records, county genealogies, and state death certificates.[1]

In the past, many predominantly white churches added notations to records of members who were African Americans ("colored" or "negro") or Native Americans to identify them as such. The South Amenia Presbyterian Church in Wassaic, New York, recorded the 1784 baptism of "Lorain, wench of Mrs. Mary Slawson," the daughter of "negro parents."[2] Some registers, such as the Saddle River, New Jersey, Dutch Reformed Church, had a separate section for "colored" records. Before the end of slavery, some church register entries (especially in the South) identified individuals as a slave or "servant," along with the slaveholder.

## Baptisms

Most Christian faiths include baptism as an essential or optional rite. Some churches baptize infants; some practice "believer's baptism" by those considered old enough to choose it. In some faiths, baptism admitted a person to a specific level of church membership. John T. Humphrey's excellent book *Understanding and Using Baptismal Records*[3] has more information on the religious significance of baptism in various faiths. The denominational chapters later in this book comment on baptism as it pertains to each faith's records.

Baptismal records may include the following information about a person:
- *Birth date and parents' names*, specifically for infant baptisms.
- *Noteworthy birth circumstances*, such as "illegitimate," "adopted," or "twin." Children born outside of marriage might also be called "natural-born" or "baseborn." Catholic records may indicate whether the event was an "emergency baptism," which would have been performed if the newborn's life was in danger at birth.
- *Siblings*. Multiple children in a single family may have been baptized on the same day, which can help identify family groups.
- *Spouse's name*, for an adult baptism (especially a woman's).
- *Other relatives or close family friends*. Witnesses, sponsors, or godparents may be mentioned; these were often relatives or others who were important to the family.
- *Probable residence* at the time of baptism and, for newborns, their likely birthplace.
- *Later life events*. Records of later Catholic rites (marriage, taking of vows) are supposed to be sent back to the parish of baptism and noted alongside the baptismal record. Well-organized Protestant churches sometimes did this as well, even across the Atlantic.

Not all children who received "infant" baptism were actually newborns. In the past, "infant" might refer to any child. Also, if a family didn't live near a resident minister or was not affiliated with a church, it may have taken months or even years for an "infant" baptism to take place. It's not uncommon to find several children from one family who received baptism at the same time. Circumstances like this and adult baptisms make it imperative to know how important infant or

1  Nathan Murphy, "Tracing German American Immigrants," 9 May 2013, *FamilySearch Blog* (https://familysearch.org/blog/en/tracing-german-american-immigrants), accessed 5 February 2019.
2  Arthur C. M. Kelly, transcriber and indexer, *Vital Records of South Amenia Presbyterian Church, Wassaic, Dutchess County, New York, 1756–1989* (Rhinebeck, N.Y.: Kinship, 2004), Part 1, Baptism record section, 19.
3  John T. Humphrey, *Understanding and Using Baptismal Records* (Washington, D.C.: Humphrey Publications, 1996).

adult baptism was to the particular church in question. Baptismal records for churches that practice believer's baptism may be less useful to genealogists.

You may find baptismal records with varying formats and content. Below are two typical examples. First is a Catholic baptismal record[4] from 1879, written in Latin (the names are also Latinized:

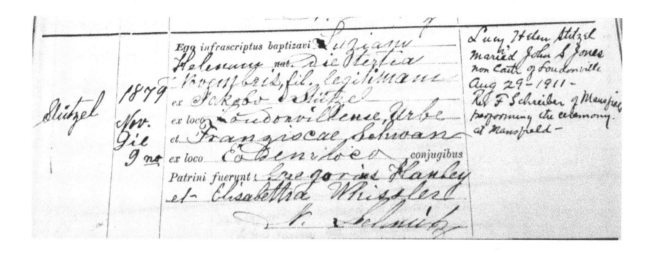

Here's what the record says:

| Surname | Baptismal date | Record entry (translation): | Comments |
|---|---|---|---|
| Slitzel (also appears in record as Stitzel) | 1879 Nov. Day 9 | I, the undersigned, baptized Lucy Helen, born 3rd day November, legitimate daughter of Jacob Slitzel from Loudonville, city and Frances Schwan from Eaden [Edentown], married couple. Godparents were Greg Hanley and Elisabeth Whissler<br><br>[Signed by priest] | Lucy Helen Stitzel married John S. Jones non Cath[olic] of Loudonville Aug 29–1911- Rev F Schreiber of Mansfield performing the ceremony at Mansfield |

On page 6 is a list of baptisms[5] performed at a United Presbyterian and Congregational Church in Ohio in the 1820s and 1830s. Entries are on a single line in a register book with columns (left to right) for the baptismal date; name of the person baptized; a parent's name, generally the father; and the minister's name. No birth dates are included, but several entries show ditto marks under the parent's name, indicating that sibling groups were baptized on the same day.

---

4  Records of St. Peter's Catholic church, Loudonville, Ashland Co., Ohio; Ohio Genealogical Society Library, Bellville, Ohio, MSS 197, File 4.

5  Baptismal records in 1817–44 record book, p. 30, United Presbyterian and Congregational Church, Farmington Twp., Trumbull Co., Ohio; MS 2125, Container 1, Folder 1, Western Reserve Historical Society, Cleveland.

## Confirmations

Some faiths include a rite of confirmation during the younger teen to adult years. This rite may qualify a person for full membership, which may include the right to receive communion (a ritual that involves the taking of bread and wine in commemoration of Jesus, participation in which may also have been noted in church records, especially if communion occurred only on special occasions).

Most confirmation records are genealogically sparse. They give the date of confirmation, name of the officiating priest, and perhaps a sponsor. But they can help place a person in a given location and time. The confirmations of several children from one family over time may be evidence of their ongoing residence there.

## Marriages

Marriages are among the most reliably kept church records, since they were both a legal and a religious event. However, the type of information recorded varied by time period and faith. For example, before the 1840s the marriage records of St. Paul's Episcopal in Albany, New York, named only the bride and groom. Later, the records sometimes listed where the bride and groom were from and witnesses' names. Not until 1906 did the clerk begin including parents' names too. In one Dutch Reformed congregation, early marriage records were sparse, but later ones included age, occupations, residences, and witnesses. The chance of finding unique details in church marriage records is a good reason to seek them out, even if you already have a civil marriage record. See Chapter 2 for an example of a church marriage record that revealed more than did the government's version.

Quaker marriage records are particularly genealogically rich. They often included the couples' names, their parents' and grandparents' names, the full marriage agreement, and the names of every person present as witnesses.

Marriage banns were "published," or read, from some church pulpits (for example, Roman Catholic, Church of England, and Lutheran) for up to three weeks before an intended marriage. In some times and places, this was required by law. Banns were meant to prevent illegal or secret marriages. The mandatory reading of banns gradually disappeared after the introduction of civil marriage license registrations, which served a similar purpose.

Mention of banns being read is often included with the church record of the actual marriage. Separate bann books in the United States are rare. The marriage record may also state permission (dispensation) to forego one or more readings of the banns for special circumstances, such as a couple about to be separated by military service, etc. Here's an example, quoted from a published transcription, with emphasis added:[6]

> The 26 June, 1843, **after the publication of one ban of marriage and the dispensation of two others** granted by us Priest Missionary, between Joseph Brunel, engagé, in the Service of the Honorable Company of Hudson's Bay in this country, of-age son of Louis Brunel and of Françoise Bellerose of the parish of Berthier of Montréal, on one part and Susanne aged about 26 years, of the nation of Cayous, in this country and of infidel parents, nor any impediment being discovered, we Priest Missionary undersigned have received their mutual consent of marriage in presence of Jean Baptiste Aubichon, among others, and of Peter Kitson, who have not known how to sign. The said spouses Joseph Brunel and Susanne having lived together in this infidel country, declare and recognize as their own child him named Louis, aged 11 years, whom they have reared. —Antoine Langlois, priest

If you do find a reference to banns without proof of the marriage event, look for evidence of the couple appearing together later in life. In some times and places, there were harsh fines if a couple didn't marry within a short time after the banns were read.

## Memberships and migrations

Many Protestant congregations kept registers of their members, which often included migration details. Here's an example from the register[7] of the First Congregational Church in Randolph, Ohio:

---

6 *Catholic Church Records of the Pacific Northwest*, Vancouver Volumes I and II and Stellamaris Mission, translated by Mikell de Lores Wormell Warner, annotated by Harriet Duncan Munnick (St. Paul, Ore.: French Prairie Press, 1972), original manuscript page 23.

7 Membership register, First Congregational Church, Randolph Twp., Portage Co., Ohio, pp. 216–7, MS 40, container 1, vol. 3, Western Reserve Historical Society, Cleveland.

The members' names appear in the left-hand column. Following are three columns under the heading "Admitted"—when, how, and whence (from where). The date refers to when the member joined the church. The "how" means the manner by which they were admitted. On this page, some were admitted "by letter," meaning they moved into town from another location and presented a letter of reference from a previous church. Others were admitted by "examination," meaning they professed their faith before representatives of the church and were found acceptable (this may also be called "profession"). "Whence" indicates a previous residence for those who transferred in by letter. Current residents who joined the church are designated as coming from the "world," meaning the secular world.

For example, the ledger on the previous page reveals that the first two listed, both named Mary, moved into town and presented letters from their previous congregations in Edinburgh (presumably Ohio, since no state is mentioned) and Evanston, Illinois. The same day, local resident Benn Ammi Allen converted to the faith by examination.

When church members moved away, the process repeated in reverse, as shown in the ledger on page 7. There are three columns under "Removed:" when, how, and where. Members in good standing were given letters dismissing them to another congregation. On this page, various members relocated in the 1880s to Rootstown and Oberlin, Ohio, and to "Huron Dakota."

It's worth clarifying here that removal, or dismission, as it's sometimes called, didn't generally mean they were expelled from denominational membership, only removed from the rolls of that particular church.

In the membership register above, there's also a helpful "Remarks" column. On the page shown, most comments identify the member's spouse. Other comments might include death, expulsion, or other information.

Membership registers vary in format and organization. In some sects, there was a probationary period before becoming a fully qualified member, so you might see separate registers for probationers and communicants (members qualified to receive communion). Some faiths listed entire family groups together on the same page; others enumerated individuals chronologically as they joined. Membership lists may be segregated by race, gender, or marital status. For example, Quaker meetings were separate for men and women and so were their records.

Membership termination may have come about by a member's voluntary withdrawal or the church's disciplinary action. Any or all of these steps may appear in church membership registers and/or minutes. There may be multiple occasions noted when various members of the congregation met privately with a "straying" member before a reconciliation or departure occurred.

Occasionally, actual letters of transfer survive in original manuscript collections of church records at archives. But they're rare. Here's an example[8] to illustrate the process of membership transfers:

---

8  Letter of dismissal issued to John Brooks 30 Aug. 1804, from the Reformed Dutch Church at Mahackemack, New York, to the Church of Jesus Christ; MS 5362, Box 3, Folder 153, Western Reserve Manuscripts (Western Reserve Historical Society Manuscript Vertical File), Western Reserve Historical Society, Cleveland.

Here's what it says: "These may certify that John Brooks is a Member in full communion of the Reformed Dutch Church at Magoghhamach, and during his residence amongst us was sound in the Faith and orderly in his walk & conversation, at least as far as we know. We therefore recommend him as such to the care and attention of the Church of Jesus Christ with whom he is now conversant. Witness our hands this 30th Augt 1804, in Consistory of the Reformed Dutch Church at Magoghhemack." Elders [signed]

## Deaths, funerals, and burials

Churches often recorded the deaths and/or burials of current and even former members. These may appear in dedicated registers of deaths; as a single column in a comprehensive membership roster; as notations in church minutes (which you'll read more about in Chapter 5); or in separate church cemetery records, if the church had its own burying ground.

Details included in death records vary widely too. A register may simply note a member's age at death, or mention that the person was "dismissed" from church membership at death (which at least tells you that person died there). Catholic burial records may mention whether the sacrament of extreme unction ("last rites") was performed. You may find notes about cause of death, place of burial, or other details.

Burial records for church cemeteries may have name and next of kin; date, place, and cause of death; the deceased's age, birthplace, marital status, and occupation; the name of the officiator;

mention of a funeral home (which may have more records!); and more. Here's a typical entry from a German church in Cincinnati, Ohio:

> Elisabeth Scheller nee Willner, born Maidingen, Amt Berne, Switzerland, May 10, 1842; died April 25, 1892. Casper Scheller, husband. [9]

Occasionally, a church register will note the burial of a member elsewhere. A body may have been returned to a family cemetery or sent to be interred with a spouse. Before the Civil War era, bodies could not be preserved and were buried wherever the person died.

Funeral sermons may provide another clue to family deaths. It's rare to find mention of these, but they are most likely to be in a minister's personal logs or diaries (more in Chapter 5).

### Participation in ministries

Many local churches kept lists of those who served in ministerial and administrative roles, with or without payment or formal training. The meaning of various terms and offices varies from one faith to the next. For more specifics, see the chapters later in this book on individual faiths.

If you have a relative who was a minister, look for church membership records kept by him or under his care (in the era covered by this book, it was almost always "him," rarely "her"). These records—whether kept as an official church register that remained with the congregation or among his private papers—may reveal the nature and duration of his ministry. For example, you may discover his date of ordination, when he began working with a particular church, or when he transferred to another. Membership records may reveal what kinds of rites he performed and how frequently, how widely he traveled, and his administrative responsibilities. They may also reveal samples of his handwriting and signature to enjoy.

Occasionally, you'll find unique annotations, such as this memorial statement from a published record of burials in a Reformed Church:

> Sept 23, 1824. Rev. Jonathan Helffenstein, the former pastor of the Hei. Ch. in Fred. He resigned his pastoral care on Sept. 6, 1828, but continued to preach a German sermon occasionally until Sabbath July 12, 1829, when he preached his last sermon. On Sept. 23, he closed the labors & sufferings of his mortal career.[10]

Churches often kept other records relating to their ministers on a regional or national level too. See Chapter 5 and the chapters on individual faiths for more information on religious newspapers, ministers' files, obituaries/memorials, etc.

## PERSONAL BELIEFS

Not everyone's church affiliation accurately reflected their personal beliefs. In colonial times, attendance at a government-supported church may have been required, and it may have been the place where all residents' vital records were kept, regardless of their faith. On the frontier, local options for religious worship were often limited. A couple may have joined a church in deference to one spouse's beliefs, which the other may not have shared. Even members who were fairly devout may not have fully embraced every tenet their church preached. But learning about the relevant churches' creeds can better inform you about the religious culture in which they lived.

---

9  Jeffrey Herbert, ed., *First German Protestant Cemetery of Avondale & Martini United Church of Christ Records;* Hamilton County, Ohio, Burial Records, vol. 13 (Cincinnati: Hamilton County Chapter of Ohio Genealogical Society, 2014), 134.

10   George Merle de Fere Zacharias, transcriber, "Transcript of Church Records 1747–1875, Evangelical Reformed Church (Frederick, Maryland)," vol. 1, 331; Family History Library [FHL] microfilm 13,935.

## WHAT TO EXPECT

Will the records you find really have all this great stuff? Maybe less. The above is just a description of what you *might* find. As a rule, the older a record, the fewer details it will have—if only because writing materials were expensive and scarce.

And then again, maybe more. In addition to what's already been described, churches may have other records that contain your family's names or shed light on their lives. There may be denominational or congregational histories, ministers' records, financial reports, donation lists, and more (see Chapter 5). The next few chapters will tell you how to find and order these all-important membership records.

*Chapter 2*

# HOW TO IDENTIFY YOUR ANCESTOR'S CHURCH

This chapter provides four approaches to locating ancestors' churches. (If you already know the answer, you can skip this chapter—at least, until you need to ask it of another ancestor.) They are listed starting with the most direct, and likely most useful, approaches:

1. Querying living relatives
2. Consulting other genealogical information on the family
3. Considering any migrations of which the family may have been a part
4. Finding churches near family residences at a given time, using county histories, historical maps, and city directories

## QUERYING LIVING RELATIVES

The most common source of knowledge *on recent generations* is the family itself. Some families have a history of attending the same parish for several generations. Other families may have diversified, but someone probably knows that great-grandma attended mass or was a lifelong Methodist.

You may have to ask this question of relatives you don't know or don't see frequently: second cousins, in-laws, great-aunts. In one case, the church was identified by cold-calling current residents of the ancestor's hometown who shared the same unusual surname. Clues may lead in the right direction without telling all: a relative may recall only an Italian-language congregation, a "holy-roller" service, or a church near the elementary school.

So ask around the family:

- Did grandma or grandpa ever attend a specific church?
- Were they ever baptized? As a child or adult?
- Where was the church?
- Was anyone in the family married in a church or buried in a church cemetery?
- Did anyone join a different church from the rest of the family?
- Did any family members ever join the clergy/religious life?
- Did anyone attend a Sunday school or a church school?

Again, don't limit inquiries to direct ancestors. Information about a sibling, cousin, aunt, or more distant relative may shed just the light you need to identify a family faith.

## CONSULT OTHER GENEALOGICAL INFORMATION ON THE FAMILY

Documents associated with someone's life may mention a church affiliation:

- *A delayed birth certificate or military benefits application* may cite (or include!) an infant baptismal record as evidence of birth.

- *Obituaries* often mention a church affiliation, a minister's name, place of services, and place of burial—all useful clues to follow.

- *Local or county histories* may mention church affiliation in a biographical sketch of a relative. Skim the section on local churches for any familiar names.

- *A government marriage record or newspaper marriage announcement* should say who married the couple. Research that minister's affiliation through his listing in a city directory, county minister's license, biography in a county history, or similar sources.

- *Other documents and artifacts*—such as funeral programs, mass cards, insurance paperwork, death certificates, iconography on a tombstone, jewelry, devotional books, family letters, and more—may point to a family's religion.

When a minister is named in a family record, try to identify the denomination and then a specific church or congregation so you can look for its records. For example, the Colorado civil marriage record of Mike Fox and Mary Eiarmann,[1] dated 28 February 1889, states that they were married by Godfrey Raeber, a Catholic priest residing at Denver:

---

1  Mike Fox-Maria Eiarmann marriage license #7123, 28 Feb. 1889, Arapahoe County Colo.; Colorado State Archives, Denver (https://www.colorado.gov/archives)>Collections>Genealogy>Marriages.

That clue led author Sunny Morton to seek out that year's *Catholic Directory*, an annual publication of the Catholic Church that listed priests' assignments. A Google search for "1889 Catholic directory" led to a digitized edition online.[2] A keyword search on "Raeber" didn't find his name, so the researcher paged through it until she came to the listings for the Diocese of Denver. The second line on this page shows that "Rev. G. Raber" (note the different spelling) was assigned to the Church of St. Ann in Northeast Denver:

DIOCESE OF DENVER. 213

North Denver, Church of St. Patrick, Rev. Jos. P. Carrigan, pastor.
Northeast Denver, Church of St. Ann, Rev. G. Raber, pastor.
South Denver, Church of St. Joseph, Rev. T. H. Malone, pastor.
Stations on the Kansas Pacific, Denver, and New Orleans and Rio Grande R. R., attended from Pro-Cathedral by Rev. —.

BOULDER COUNTY.

Boulder City (P.O.), Church of the Sacred Heart, Rev. Rhabanus Gutman, O.S.B., pastor; Revs. E. Geiger, O.S.B., Henry Hohman, O.S.B., assistants.
Erie, Caribou,
Louisville (P.O.), Church of St. Louis,
South Boulder, Church of the Sacred Heart of Mary, } attended from Boulder.
Marshall,

LARIMER COUNTY.

Fort Collins (P.O.), Church of the Immaculate Conception, Rev. Peter Robinet, pastor.
Longmont, Church of St. John, attended from Fort Collins.
Loveland, Laport, Stout, attended from Fort Collins.
Brighton (P.O.), new brick church, Rev. J. G. Hickey, pastor.
Platteville, attended from Brighton.
Stations on B. and M. R. R., attended from Brighton.
Sterling, Rev. W. J. Howlett.
Julesburg and stations on U. P. Short Line attended from Sterling.
Yuma, Akron, attended from Brighton.

WELD COUNTY.

Greely (P.O.), Church of St. Peter, attended from Fort Collins.

JEFFERSON COUNTY.

Golden City (P.O.), Church of St. Joseph, Rev. G. M. Morton, pastor.
Morrison (P.O.), Church of the Sacred Heart, Rev. D. Pantanella, S.J., pastor.

A subsequent Google search for "Catholic Church St. Ann Denver Colorado" didn't bring up any current parishes, so Sunny googled the contact information for the Diocese of Denver's archivist. She learned that Denver now has an Archdiocese. She called its archivist and asked about the status of the Church of St. Ann's and the current whereabouts of its parish records. The parish had closed, and the archivist had the parish records. Sunny paid a fee, and he emailed her a copy of the marriage record:

The first column is a line number, followed by the marriage date. Then appears information for the groom, Mike Fox: his name, age (23); marriage number (1); residence (Denver); names of father and mother (Martin and Francis); and birthplace (Germany). Similar details appear for the bride, Mary Eairrman. Only the couple's Denver residence appears in the civil marriage record; the rest of these details are unique to the church record.

---

2 *Sadliers' Catholic Directory Almanac and Ordo for the Year of Our Lord 1889* (New York: D. & J. Sadlier & Co., 1889), 213.

To try a similar technique, consult the denominational chapters in this book or contact church archivists to learn about any annual publications comparable to the *Catholic Directory* that would contain ministerial assignments for that time period. You might also see whether a church archive has files on ministers that would mention the assigned church (or churches) during the time period in question. Then you could look for that church's records.

## CONSIDER ANY MIGRATIONS

In colonial times and during the "frontier era" of each region (and sometimes beyond), there was much less religious diversity than there is today. Knowing where relatives were at particular times may hint at a religious affiliation (even if it was a matter of convenience or compulsion). Consider whether one of the following situations might have applied to your family:

### Colonial-established churches

Some colonial governments enforced an established faith. Local churches of these faiths often served semi-governmental roles, including keeping vital records and records of taxes paid to them (which the law may have required of all residents, no matter their personal beliefs). Below are four examples:

- Spanish and French colonists in areas later annexed to the United States were largely Catholic.
- Settlers in New York and New Jersey often left records in the Dutch Reformed Church.
- Early New Englanders were supposed to attend Congregationalist churches.
- In the South, English settlers were most likely to appear in records of the Anglican Church (Church of England).

After these churches were disestablished, their strength in the colonies-turned-states lessened, though in many regions it still hasn't entirely disappeared. During the Second Great Awakening (late 1700s and early 1800s), popular religious tastes in the United States moved toward churches with more emotional, democratic, and "can-do" messages.

### Settlers' preferences

As new migrant groups arrived in an area, they brought their churches with them (see the map below). For example, Scandinavian settlers popularized Lutheranism in Minnesota and the Dakotas. Mormon pioneers created a strong Latter-day Saint presence in Utah and Idaho. If your ancestor was part of such a migration, it may suggest a religious affiliation. This trend may be strongest at the time an area was first settled by those of European descent but may also apply to later or smaller waves of arrivals. And in some cases emigrants may have been dissenters in their homeland, or part of a division within the faith later on. Sometimes a family's migration provided a perfect opportunity to leave behind an unwanted affiliation. This may have occurred immediately, or it may have taken the family a generation or two to change its religious identity.

Many who moved westward found a home with the Baptists and Methodists. Their messages appealed to the democratic spirit of many frontier settlers. Preachers were willing to travel hundreds of miles on a circuit to visit scattered followers, who appreciated the attention but didn't demand large or continuous investment from church officials. Methodists were especially strong in the Midwest. Both Methodists and Baptists did well in the Appalachian regions, along with Presbyterians. Baptists had greatest saturation in the South.

## Dominant Religious Groups at Time of European Settlement

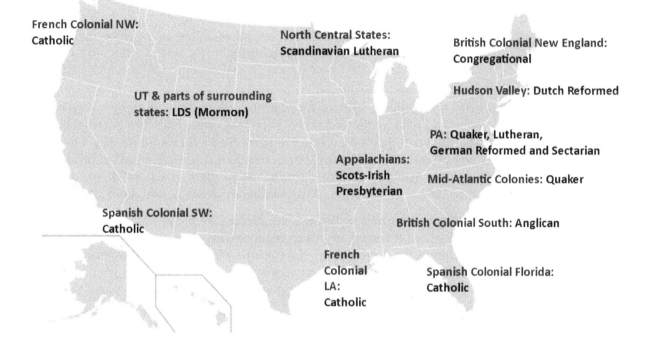

### Immigrant churches

Many immigrants and the generation or two who followed them chose where to worship along ethnic or nation-of-origin lines. Scots-Irish arrivals were largely Presbyterians. Many French who settled in Pennsylvania and Virginia were Huguenots. Many Germans and Scandinavians were Lutherans. (German immigrants had some of the greatest religious diversity, with considerable numbers of Jews, Catholics, and other faiths.) Irish and Italian immigrants were predominantly Catholic, as were many Poles, Slovaks, and other Eastern Europeans.

Many European immigrants settled in large cities or labor markets among others of their national or ethnic origin. This helped many families maintain their native religions, and it can help you locate their churches easily. After the mid-1800s, Catholics frequently organized parishes for specific ethnic or language groups.

African immigrants' spiritual beliefs were forcibly repressed under slavery. However, many of them or their enslaved descendants eventually converted to Christianity, whether voluntarily or not. The baptisms of enslaved African Americans may appear among the records of a slave-holder's church. A handful of free African-American churches existed before emancipation. After the Civil War, hundreds and eventually thousands of African-American churches were formed, largely in the Methodist or Baptist traditions.

As a family's ethnic identity faded over the generations, so may have its loyalty to a specific church. Descendants lost personal connection with language and culture, moved to new places, met and married outside the faith, joined other churches, or left religion behind altogether.

## USE COUNTY HISTORIES, HISTORICAL MAPS, AND CITY DIRECTORIES

It's also possible to search from the opposite direction: look at local or neighborhood records to see exactly which churches were in town, then form an educated guess. (Of course, this technique works better for those times and places where a twenty-mile trip was a major obstacle to attendance!) For example, if there were Greek Orthodox and Irish Roman Catholic parishes within three blocks of your family's home, a black Methodist church across the river, and a Presbyterian church downtown, which would your relatives likely have attended?

These days, it's possible to discover contemporary local churches online, using three main tools: local and county histories, historical maps, and city directories.

## Local and county histories

Local and county histories are excellent sources for learning when early churches were established, who attended them, and who ministered there. They may cover churches before the mid-1800s and smaller churches that may not have created or preserved their own histories. There are both paper and digital avenues to finding either paper or digital histories. A standard print reference is Filby's *A Bibliography of American County Histories*.[3] Some states, such as Michigan, have collected and digitized these books and even made it possible to search across them all.

A general web search on the names of the county and state, along with the phrase "county history," may bring up many (but not all) of the same results as the following more targeted strategies. Remember that keyword-searching a digitized version of a county history is almost always easier than searching the original un-indexed paper version—but keyword searches don't always find everything. If you're searching a digitized version, enjoy the convenience, but then read its pages too.

- The Library of Congress has an online portal to arguably the most comprehensive catalog of U.S. local histories (http://www.loc.gov/rr/genealogy/tips.html). Follow the county history search tips on the site for best results. Titles will likely not be borrowable, so once you've found a good match, search for a digital version online or a borrowable copy in WorldCat (see below).

- WorldCat (http://www.worldcat.org) is the best source for finding potentially borrowable copies of county histories or copies. Keyword searches (e.g., "Franklin County Ohio history") are pretty effective: do these from the Advanced Search screen. Better yet, once you've found one relevant title, scroll down the catalog entry to the subject terms. Click on the county history subject term, formatted like this: "Bosque County (Tex.)—History." That will bring up all other titles tagged with that subject term. (Learn more about using WorldCat and the other resources in Chapter 3.)

- If you're coming up dry in WorldCat, perhaps because of not having the right keywords, try the FamilySearch Catalog (https://www.familysearch.org/catalog/search). This catalog is organized geographically and then by record type, so you can search for all histories within a given county. Search by place down to the county level, then look for the category "History." Digitized versions of county histories will have links in the catalog entry. If you find a print book that's not borrowable, search for a copy through WorldCat or in online digital archives (see below).

- Online digital archives are a great place to find old county histories, since copyright has expired for many. Search Google Books (https://books.google.com), Internet Archive (https://archive.org), HathiTrust Digital Archive (https://www.hathitrust.org), Digital Public Library of America (https://dp.la/), and state-specific digital archives.

County histories are found in genealogical libraries of all sizes. Some histories lack every-name indexes; others are accompanied by separately bound indexes created at a later date.

## Historical maps

Historical maps often identify churches by name and location. Look for maps from around the time period your family lived in a certain location, as early churches could disappear or change names over time.

---

3  P. William Filby, comp., *A Bibliography of American County Histories* (1985; repr., Baltimore: Genealogical Publishing Co., 2009).

Maps may be available at county or city government offices, archives, or in the collections of local libraries, societies, colleges, or universities. Maps also appear in published histories and atlases (use the same finding tools as described above), city directories (see below), and digital archives like the Library of Congress's Map Collection (https://www.loc.gov/collection/cities-and-towns/about-this-collection/) and the David Rumsey Historical Map Collection (https://www.davidrumsey.com/).

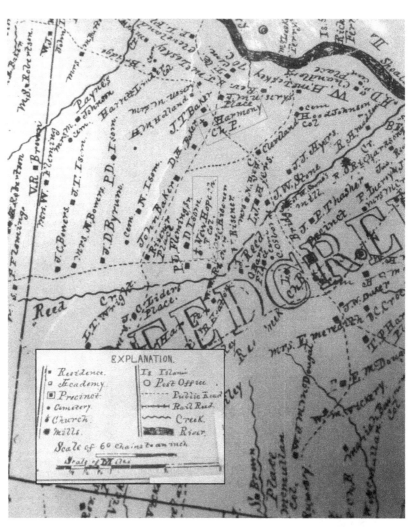

This 1889 hand-drawn map of Reed Creek, Hart County, Georgia,[4] isn't easy to read. But the map key (see inset) shows that churches are marked by a dot with a cross on top. Marked in this image for easier viewing are two churches: "New Hope Ch. B Col," (likely meaning "New Hope Church, Baptist, Colored") and "Harmony Ch, P" (Presbyterian?), which in the absence of a racial designation likely meant a church for white people.

Sanborn fire insurance maps also are fantastic resources for the cities and towns of the late 1800s and early 1900s. These detailed neighborhood-level maps were created for city planners and insurers. Businesses, churches, and other organizations are often labeled. The 1888 Sanborn Fire Insurance Map[5] on the next page includes a section of C Street S.W., just east of Sixth Street, in Washington, D.C. Three churches appear in this little neighborhood: the Sixth Presbyterian Church, Fifth Baptist Church, and St. John's German Lutheran Church.

## City directories

City directories were the precursors to telephone books, and equally ephemeral. They are most available for the mid-1800s and beyond. Directories for major urban areas may reach back to the early 1800s or even late 1700s, but smaller towns have few until the late 1800s or early 1900s. In many times and places, directories were published annually. They listed households, businesses, government agencies, societies, schools, and community organizations such as churches. Many had a dedicated section for churches. Occasionally, larger places even had competing directories: check both!

---

4   J.W. Baker, *General Description Map of Hart County*, Ga. (N.p.: privately published, 1889).
5   *Insurance Map of Washington [D.C.]* (New York: Sanborn Map Publishing Co., 1888), 7 (https://www.loc.gov/resource/g3851gm.g3851gm_g012271888/?sp=7).

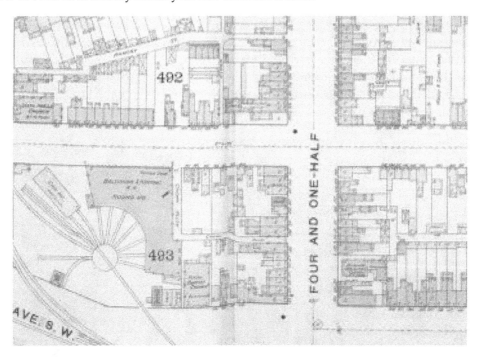

The 1861 Detroit directory, digitized on Ancestry[6] (https://www.ancestry.com/), actually has a separate section listing all the churches in the city:

6   *1861 Johnston's Detroit City Directory* (Detroit: James Dale Johnston & Co., 1861), 32–33; "U.S. City Directories, 1822–1995" > Michigan > Detroit > 1861 > Detroit, Michigan, City Directory, 1861 > image 27 of 188 (Ancestry.com).

Ancestry has an enormous but incomplete collection of U.S. city directories. Under the Search tab, select "Card Catalog," then sort the results by "record count" and "U.S. City Directories, 1822–1995" will appear at the top of the list. Click on it and choose the option to browse. Choose the locale, then the year, to page through a specific directory. The search function may pull up particular names of people or institutions.

Another resource for locating directories is City Directories of the United States of America (http://www.uscitydirectories.com). Search by location and the record type "city directory." You will learn what range of years is available and see a few libraries' lists of holdings. Go to World-Cat to find more libraries with the right editions. Local public libraries and historical and genealogical societies usually have copies of their past city directories too. They may be the only holders for smaller towns and for earlier dates in the small towns.

The Allen County Public Library Genealogy Center's Microtext Catalog (http://www.genealogy center.info/search_microtext.php) is another resource that bypasses some of the quirky ways libraries may catalog physical city directories. The collection is not complete, but few libraries can match its scope of coverage beyond its own local area in both physical and microfilm versions.

Once you find a directory, go to the beginning and look to see if the contents page includes a section on the city's churches. If you can keyword-search the directory, search for the word "church."

Between the addresses and maps, you may be able to locate most of a town's or neighborhood's churches. If you have a pastor's name from a marriage record, baptismal certificate, or obituary, you may also be able to use directories to identify the church with which he was affiliated. Try scanning through any special section for churches or ministers—or look up the minister's name in the residential part of the directory.

## MORE POSSIBILITIES

Helpful in this phase of research, and later, are geographical or ethnic-based resources. Two good examples:

- Wardell J. Payne's *Directory of African American Religious Bodies* has over 1,000 listings of religious bodies and their structure, membership and dogma, and a helpful glossary of terms.[7]
- The New York Genealogical and Biographical Society's *New York Family History Research Guide and Gazetteer* includes a generous section on "Religious Records of New York" including Baptist, Catholic, Congregational, Eastern Rite and Eastern Orthodox, Episcopal, Jewish, Lutheran, Methodist, Latter-day Saint, Presbyterian, Quaker, and Reformed.[8]

7   Wardell J. Payne, ed., *Directory of African-American Religious Bodies: A Compendium by the Howard University School of Divinity*, 2nd ed. (Washington, D.C.: Howard University Press, 1995).
8   *New York Family History Research Guide and Gazetteer*, rev. ed. (New York: New York Genealogical and Biographical Society, 2017).

*Chapter 3*

---

# HOW TO FIND AND ORDER CHURCH RECORDS

---

Once you've determined where your family likely attended church, how can you find that church's records?

In many faiths, records are supposed to be maintained at the local church office. So theoretically, all you have to do is contact the right church office. However, the church your ancestors attended may have closed or merged with another church. Records may have been forwarded to the successor church or to a central church archive. In some cases, you may need to follow the history of a denomination forward to locate the right church archive. (See "Help! What Church Is This Now?" later in this chapter, and the chapters on individual denominations later in this book.)

Extant records may also have ended up in archives at a nearby historical society or college or university. In states that had established churches during colonial times, church records may be at state archives. Records may even be buried in an apparently unrelated archive far from home. For example, records from the Baptist church in Montville, Connecticut, are now at the Western Reserve Historical Society in Cleveland, Ohio (which makes sense once you know that Connecticut residents helped to settle that part of Ohio).

This chapter describes (and then summarizes) several different approaches to finding original, published, or imaged church records. The path to follow may be simple or convoluted. Sometimes a search for one type of record (say, original records) leads to another (say, a published index).

## SEARCH FOR ORIGINAL RECORDS AT CHURCH OFFICES

If an ancestor's congregation still exists, you may be able to find it—or its successor church—quickly with a Google search. For example, a Google search for "Methodist Church Linn Creek Missouri" brings up contact information for a local congregation.

Few church websites answer key genealogical questions, such as whether the congregation existed at the time your relative lived there, whether it has records from that time period (and how to request copies of them), or where else those records may be, if they exist. Use the contact information online to call or email the office and ask. See the individual denominational chapters later in this book for links to online congregation locator tools.

Before contacting a church, it's worth reflecting on the fact that churches are private institutions with no obligation to let anyone see their records. Freedom of information laws and regulations do not apply. Many of the denominations discussed in this book are no longer growing and flourishing as in the past; in some cases, pastoral offices must weigh attention to their proud history against the needs of living parishioners. Show respect for their ministerial priorities and state your willingness to wait your turn. Offer to send a donation to the church or pay for a researcher's time.

It may not be easy to get a response from the office, and the response may be reluctant. Many church offices are run by minimal and/or volunteer staff. Even if you speak with someone, they may ask for a written request. But even a brief telephone conversation can confirm whether you are requesting the right record from the right place and using the right procedure (including any fee that should be sent ahead of time).

## Checklist: ordering records from congregational offices

✓ Call ahead and/or check the website to see a) whether this is likely the right church, b) whether they have the records you need, and c) whether there are special instructions and/or a special form they require.

✓ Be brief and specific. Tell them everything they need to know to process your request— *and nothing they don't need to know*. If you have a long list of records to request, start with (at most) the four or five most important. (Bear in mind that a request for a search over a period of years may be much more laborious to fulfill than one pinpointed to a specific time.) Send a follow-up request only after seeing how the first one goes.

✓ Send a check with your order. If fees are not stated, send $25 to $40 in a check made out to the church. Offer to send additional reimbursement for copying and mailing expenses if needed.

✓ Specify that you would like copies of the original records, if possible. If they must transcribe the information onto a pre-printed certificate instead, ask them to include *every piece of information about that person*, not just what the certificate has room for. (This is also good advice if you are fortunate enough to view and transcribe the original records themselves!)

✓ Include your email address (or contact information if the office is not equipped for email), in case they have questions or need to send digital images.

✓ Thank them in advance for their response.

## Sample letter: to request copies of records

*Dear Pastoral Office,*

*I am seeking copies of membership records for early members of your church who were my ancestors. As your time and staffing permit, will you please search your old records and send copies of the following records:*

1. ***Thomas Selby—church membership/baptism** (1870s–1880s) and **death record** (died 7 April 1886)*

2. *His wife **Hulda (Wilbur) Selby**—**church membership/baptism** (1870s–1880s) and **death record** (died 17 March 1896)*

3. ***Fannie Selby—birth and baptism** (born 14 May 1867) and **death record** (23 September 1867)*

*Please send photocopies of original records, if possible. If only certificates/typed information are to be sent, please include any and all information about each person's birth date/age, birthplace, relatives' names and relationships, residence, dates of baptism, church affiliation(s), cause of death, etc.*

*Enclosed is a donation for the church to cover expenses and express my thanks. Please advise me if additional payment is required.*

*Thank you for your time,*
*Gene E. Olgyst (include your address, phone, and email)*

There are times you will strike out—when nobody responds, or they tell you the church's old records no longer exist. In the latter case, follow up with the denomination's regional church archivist to confirm and possibly seek a new direction.

## SEARCH AT CHURCH AND OTHER ARCHIVES

Many denominations have regional or centralized archives. For instance, Catholics have diocesan and archdiocesan archives; Methodists have archives for each regional conference. See the denominational chapters in the second half of this book for more information about church archives.

Church archivists, whether volunteer or professional, full or part time,

- often have or know of records for defunct congregations and for those that have given up stewardship of their old records;
- can frequently help you follow the history of a specific congregation forward in time to identify its current name and contact information, or whether it closed or merged with another congregation;
- sometimes know where a congregation's records are (especially merged ones), even if the archives don't have them; and
- often know of other useful records, such as denominational newspapers, histories, or ministerial records (see the relevant denominational chapter).

Regional or central church archives are more likely than individual churches to have websites with instructions for genealogical research requests, standard fees and/or forms, and email contact information. You may find at least a general description of holdings, a searchable catalog, or online finding aids (descriptive materials for specific manuscript collections). Try to learn as much as possible online before contacting an archivist/librarian for assistance. Again, they likely have limited time and appreciate informed questions.

See the chapters on specific denominations later in this book for more suggestions. For those not covered in this book, try the following:

- The annual *Yearbook of American and Canadian Churches*.[1]
- *Preliminary Guide to Church Records Repositories*.[2] This dated descriptive catalog of repositories is organized by denomination, from Advent Christian to Universalist.
- *A Survey of American Church Records: Major Denominations before 1880*.[3]

Denominational archives do not always have a monopoly on old church records; some are now in private, university, or government archives. Collections may have been donated before a centralized church archive was created, or before it was standard policy to send the records there. Some churches are affiliated with universities or colleges and house their records there. Some government archives, such as the Maryland State Archives (https://msa.maryland.gov/), have church records, especially for the colonial era and for state-supported churches. Some universities have good collections or at least online resources, such as the University of Delaware's genealogy webpage for church records (from the home page at https://library.udel.edu, click on the Research tab, then choose Research Guides > Genealogy & Biography > Genealogy > Church Records).

1  National Council of the Churches of Christ in the U.S.A., *Yearbook of American and Canadian Churches* (Nashville: Abingdon Press [1916–2012]). A current version is available at http://www.yearbookofchurches.org.
2  August Robert Suelflow, *Preliminary Guide to Church Records Repositories* (St. Louis, Mo.: Society of American Archivists, Church Archives Committee, 1969).
3  E. Kay Kirkham, *A Survey of American Church Records: Major and Minor Denominations before 1880–1890*, 4th ed. (Logan, Utah: Everton, 1978).

Some original church records are cataloged at WorldCat (https://www.worldcat.org/). But separate online multi-repository catalogs have been created specifically for searching for original records held in archives. You should especially know about these three:

- **ArchiveGrid** (https://researchworks.oclc.org/archivegrid/) is a multi-library database of over 3 million archival materials held at thousands of libraries, museums, societies, and archives. This database includes entries from NUCMC, the National Union Catalog of Manuscript Collections (see below). ArchiveGrid is user-friendly. If you find a promising catalog entry but can't tell where it's from, try searching the public interface of NUCMC or ask your favorite research librarian for help.

- **NUCMC** stands for the National Union Catalog of Manuscript Collections, a master inventory of original manuscript items that has been updated annually since 1959. In 1986 annual updates started being added to WorldCat. Now you can search a Library of Congress portal to just those items at http://www.loc.gov/coll/nucmc/oclcsearch.html. Follow the instructions for the simple or advanced search options. This search interface isn't very attractive or user-friendly. You'll need to take an extra step or two to identify where the item you want is held (the site tells you how). If you want to search items cataloged by NUCMC between 1959 and 1985, you'll need to locate the annual printed catalogs or use Archive Finder (see below). Learn more about NUCMC at https://www.loc.gov/coll/nucmc/searchingfaqs.html.

- **Archive Finder/ArchivesUSA.** This subscription-only directory catalogs more than 220,000 collections of archival materials in thousands of repositories. It includes everything in the NUCMC since its inception in 1959 as well as two other major inventories of archival collections: the Directory of Archives and Manuscript Resources in the United States (DAMRUS) and the National Inventory of Documentary Sources in the United States, originally a ProQuest microfiche series. Ask whether this is available to you (or to the research librarian) at your favorite library.

These three overlap but each contains pointers to materials that the other two do not.

It is also worth checking the online catalogs of state archives, libraries, and historical and genealogical societies. Follow up with a phone call if it appears their archival collections aren't fully cataloged online. Call or email smaller societies that don't have complete online catalogs.

Print inventories and directories of old church records may be harder to come by, but just the resource you need. Look for guides such as the following in major genealogical research libraries:

- *Searching for American Church Records,*[4] with record collections organized by state.
- *Directory of Maryland Church Records,*[5] with the denomination, year span of records and the archive that holds the records. (Ask a reference librarian about comparable guides for other states.)
- WPA church record inventories. See a separate section on these later in this chapter.

## FIND PUBLISHED, IMAGED, AND INDEXED RECORDS
### Digitized images and/or indexes of church records

Digitized images and/or indexes of church records have been published on major genealogy websites by the millions. As of this writing, the largest collections for U.S. churches are at Ancestry and include Quaker, Evangelical Lutheran Church of America, Dutch Reformed, and United Methodist (and some predecessor denominations) records. Findmypast (https://www.findmypast.com/) has a growing archive of Catholic records. FamilySearch (https://familysearch.org) has a growing number of church marriage record indexes by state and some imaged records,

---

4   Fran Carter-Walker, *Searching American Church Records* (Indianapolis: Ye Olde Genealogie Shoppe, 2003).
5   Edna A. Kanely, *Directory of Maryland Church Records* (Silver Spring, Md.: Family Line Publications, 1987).

which are sometimes found in compiled vital record collections rather than in collections specific to a church or denomination.

Few denominations have published large collections of early congregational records online. A notable exception is the Congregational Library & Archives in Boston (http://www.congrega tionallibrary.org/). Learn more about specific collections and other online resources in the denominational chapters later in this book.

Use multiple strategies to search for online images and indexes, depending on what you already know, in order to capture results you may miss otherwise. Choose search terms that will help you find the following:

- *References to records of specific congregations.* Use the name of the congregation, denomination, town/state, and the keyword "records." For example, the search "Bradford MA Church of Christ records" brings up materials at the Congregational Library website. Another search for "Brooklyn NY Catholic Church records" brings up a collection available at Ancestry.

- *All church records for a specific locality.* Use the name of the city, county, and state and the keyword phrase "church records." This may help you find records for churches you didn't know about or whose names may be different than you expected. It can help when you aren't sure what church your relatives attended and want to see what options are within easy reach.

- *All church records for a particular denomination and/or state.* This wide-ranging search may point you toward collections of a broader scope. Your family's church may be included in these but not named specifically, so an online search for just the congregation's name might miss these collections.

## Microfilmed and/or published transcripts of original church records

These are still much more commonly available than online digital versions:

- *Microfilmed records* from the Family History Library in Salt Lake City, Utah (cataloged online in the FamilySearch Catalog) are no longer loaned out. They are rapidly being digitized, as contract permissions allow. Digitized films have several different levels of online access, ranging from those that can be viewed by anyone on any computer, up to those viewable only at the Family History Library. Consult the FamilySearch Catalog (https://www.familysearch.org/search/catalog/search) for the current status of specific record collections. (Search by location and then by record type to identify all church records for a given locale.) Some filmed records are also available from state, church, or other repositories via interlibrary loan.

- *Published transcripts* are available for the records of many churches, especially those with records dating to the 1700s or even 1600s. Easy to read and search, these may be borrowable through interlibrary loan. But they may be incomplete or inaccurate too. Read more about working with published records in Chapter 4.

Search for both kinds of records at WorldCat (http://www.worldcat.org), a free catalog with over two billion items from over 10,000 libraries, including the Family History Library in Salt Lake City. You don't even have to create a login unless you want to create your own reading or research lists or write reviews.

To search from the main search box on the WorldCat home page, enter a title or use the same kinds of keywords you would in a web browser search. Start with a keyword search with the name of the denomination and/or congregation, town, and state. Play around with the search terms: if "Anglican" doesn't bring up any results, use "Episcopalian." Consult the denominational chapters later in this book to see what keywords apply to that faith.

For a more targeted or detailed search, use the Advanced Search option. This will let you distinguish between words in a title, an author's name, and keywords, as well as target specific types of results (such as microfilmed content).

If you don't find what you're looking for, broaden your search. Try dropping the name of the specific congregation (which may have changed or may appear in slightly different form). A search of just the denomination and location may bring up congregations you didn't know about.

If you find a record, click on it for the full entry. You'll see the record and a description of it. Descriptions of the record type are sometimes a little confusing or inconsistent. For example, all three copies in WorldCat for "New Windsor Presbyterian Church record, Marriages and baptisms 1774–1796" are described as "archival materials." You have to look even further below in the record to clarify that this entry is for a typewritten transcript, not the original manuscript.

You'll also see a list of libraries that have this item. Sort by the ones nearest you and then link to the library website to contact a librarian and see whether the item can be borrowed through interlibrary loan to a library near you. If you're borrowing a microfilm, make sure you have it sent to a library near you that has microfilm readers.

You can also search by subject classification in WorldCat. Since supplying a list of all possible subject classifications is beyond the scope of this book, here's a quick strategy for finding them. Look for church record catalog entries that are similar to what you hope to find, either by denomination or location. Then look down at their subject headers in the catalog entry. For example, the Bush River Baptist Church Record's subject headers are "Baptists—South Carolina" and "United States, South Carolina, Newberry, Bush River—Church records." Clicking on either or both of these subjects will lead you to other titles classified that way. Clicking on "Similar items" (just below the subjects) will give you additional related subjects.

## Church record transcriptions or indexes published in journals

Transcriptions or indexes published in journals are often overlooked. You may come across them while searching online for digitized records or published books. But you're most likely to find them if you look in PERSI.

PERSI is the PERiodical Source Index, with over 2.5 million entries from thousands of genealogical, historical, and related periodicals. PERSI article coverage spans the globe but is strongest for the United States. Articles are all indexed the way a family historian needs them: by place and by important keywords, such as the name of a church or minister. (Unfortunately, it is primarily a subject index and does not index every name in each article.)

PERSI can be searched at the subscription site Findmypast, whether or not you are a subscriber. Access PERSI directly via https://search.findmypast.com/search/periodical-source-index or from the home page (Search > Newspapers & Periodicals > Periodical Source Index). Over 96,000 articles in this database are classified solely as church records; many thousands more include church records as a subject.

To search PERSI, enter the keywords of interest in the Who, Where, and What Else search boxes at the top of the screen. The Who category is appropriate for a minister's surname (because it's a subject index, your ancestors' names will only show up in PERSI if there's an article about them). In the Where search box, enter the locale. In the What Else search box, enter the name of a church or denomination, if known, or even just the word "church."

After getting your search results, narrow them down by using the filtering options along the left side of the screen. Hint: you can choose "church records" as a subject category.

Findmypast subscribers can open search results to see more specific information about each entry, such as the issue and page numbers of the article. In a growing number of search results, you will also find full-text versions of the article itself. If you aren't logged in as a subscriber, the results list will likely just show you the article title, periodical title, and the year (not the issue). In some cases, that may be sufficient for you to use other means to find that article's full citation information (try a Google search on the article, or a personal search of online or offline issues). You can also either

- purchase a Findmypast subscription or PayAsYouGo credits for à la carte access to just the records you choose (learn more at https://www.findmypast.com/subscribe); or
- head to your nearest satellite Family History Center, which you can find at https://www.familysearch.org/locations, and access the site through their online portal.

If you find an article of interest but don't have access to the article itself, the easiest option is usually to request a copy through the Allen County Public Library's Article Fulfillment service (http://www.genealogycenter.org; under Services, choose "Article Fulfillment Form"). There's a minimal fee for ordering copies of up to six articles at a time.

## SEE WHETHER WPA RESOURCES EXIST

During the Great Depression in the late 1930s and early 1940s, the federal government employed people to inventory historical records in each state as part of the Works Progress Administration (later Work Projects Administration), commonly known as the WPA. Church records were among those inventoried.

Different kinds of inventories were done in each state, some as part of a federal survey of church records and some as part of state-level transcription projects. According to one source,[6] directories of churches and religious organizations were created for twenty-five states; church archive inventory projects were undertaken in an overlapping twenty-seven states. You may also find guides to church vital statistics records for some places.

Each of these resources may differ in format and content. One state's church archives inventory form requests the church name(s), address, pastor name, details about the building(s), race and size of congregation, location of church records, and other relevant information. There's a section for a brief history of the church, and for a description of existing records and where they were located at that time.

As in the case of other WPA projects, not every project was completed statewide or for all denominations. Projects were not uniformly carried out or completed, and some of those completed were never collected or maintained by any national agency. Some were published, and some are now online. You may find a published or unpublished inventory for a single county, a single denomination within a state, or for all churches in the state. The information they contain is about seventy-five years out of date but is closer in time to the pre-1900 years this book focuses on. An increasing number of these resources are within reach, thanks to online cataloging and digitization. Like city directories, these WPA compilations are often cataloged differently by different libraries and archives.

The list in the table on pages 30–33 represents the most current and comprehensive compilation of WPA church directories and church record inventories known. For easy access, readers are directed to digitized versions online. See WorldCat for physical library holdings. Additional digitized publications will likely surface; we encourage you to search for them even if not listed here.

---

6   Bryan L. Mulcahy, "Works Progress Administration Historical Records Survey," 14 Mar. 2011, 12–13 (http://sites.rootsweb.com/~flmgs/articles/Works_Projects_AdministrationMarch2011_BM.pdf).

## WPA Church Inventories

### General resources

| | |
|---|---|
| **Multistate** | The University of Oklahoma Western History Collections (https://libraries.ou.edu/content/westernhistory-collections-0) has a multistate Historical Records Survey Collection that spans 33 states; finding aid at https://libraries.ou.edu/locations/docs/westhist/pdf/wpahistoricalrecordssurvey.pdf. |
| **African American** | *Directory of Negro Baptist Churches in the United States.* 2 vols. Digitized at HathiTrust.org. |

### Resources by state

| | |
|---|---|
| **Alabama** | *Guide to Vital Statistics Records in Alabama Church Archives, 1942.* Available at the Family History Library, Salt Lake City, Utah. |
| | *An Inventory of the Protestant Episcopal Church Archives for Alabama.* Digitized at https://exploreuk. uky.edu/ and in Multistate collection, above. |
| **Alaska** | None (not a state yet). |
| **Arizona** | *Directory of Churches and Religious Organizations in Arizona.* Digitized at HathiTrust.org. |
| **Arkansas** | *Directory of Churches and Religious Organizations in the State of Arkansas.* Digitized at http://libinfo.uark.edu/specialcollections/wpa/msh62.asp. |
| | *Guide to Vital Statistics Records in Arkansas* (church records inventory in vol. 2). Digitized at HathiTrust.org. |
| **California** | *Directory of Churches and Religious Organizations* for San Francisco, Los Angeles County, Alameda County, San Diego County, and Southern California, all in Multistate collection, above. |
| | *A Guide to Church Vital Statistics Records in California* (San Francisco and Alameda Counties: Six Denominations). Digitized at FamilySearch.org and HathiTrust.org. |
| **Colorado** | *Inventory of the Church Archives of Colorado,* Jewish Bodies. Digitized at HathiTrust.org. |
| **Connecticut** | *Inventory of the Church Archives of Connecticut* for Protestant Episcopal and Lutheran Churches. In Multistate collection, above. Protestant Episcopal republished as *Historical Resources of the Episcopal Dioceses of Connecticut.* |
| | *Guide to Vital Statistics in the Church Records of Connecticut.* Digitized at FamilySearch.org. |
| **Delaware** | *Directory of Churches and Religious Organizations in Delaware.* Digitized at HathiTrust.org. |
| | *Inventory of the Church Archives of Delaware.* Digitized at HathiTrust.org and https://archives.delaware.gov/wp-content/uploads/sites/156/2016/10/WPAChurchArchives.pdf. |
| **District of Columbia** | *Directory of Churches and Religious Organizations in the District of Columbia.* Digitized at Ancestry. com (subscription required). |
| | *Inventories of Church Archives in the District of Columbia and Inventories of Records of St. Patrick's Church and School.* |
| **Florida** | Church records inventory at Florida Memory, searchable at http://www.floridamemory.com/collections/churchrecords/. |
| | *A Preliminary List of Religious Bodies in Florida.* Digitized at HathiTrust.org. |
| | *Guide to Supplementary Vital Statistics from Church Records in Florida,* vols. 1 and 2. Digitized at FamilySearch.org. |
| **Georgia** | *Inventory of the Church Archives of Georgia.* In Multistate collection, above. |
| **Hawaii** | None (not a state yet). |

**Resources by state (*continued*)**

| | |
|---|---|
| Idaho | *Directory of Churches and Religious Organizations of Idaho.* Available at several libraries; see WorldCat.org. Digitized at HathiTrust.org. |
| Illinois | *Guide to Church Vital Statistics Records in Illinois.* Digitized at HathiTrust.org.<br><br>*Inventory of the Church Archives of Illinois,* various volumes. |
| Indiana | *A Directory of Churches and Religious Organizations in Indiana.* 3 vols. Vol. 1 (Indianapolis and Marion County), digitized at HathiTrust.org. Vol. 2, Calumet Region, Lake, Porter, and La Porte counties in Multistate collection, above. Vol. 3, Northern Indiana in Multistate collection, above. |
| Iowa | *Survey of State and Local Historical Records, 1936: Church Records* [Iowa]. FHL microfilm 1,907,246, item 3.<br><br>For extensive description of survey process, Trudy Huskamp Peterson, "The Iowa Historical Records Survey, 1936–1942," *The American Archivist* (April 1974), 223–45. Digitized at http://americanarchivist.org/doi/pdf/10.17723/aarc.37.2.n435222750xj0129. |
| Kansas | None known. |
| Kentucky | *A Preliminary Bibliography Relating to Churches in West Virginia, Virginia, Kentucky, and Southern Ohio.* Digitized at HathiTrust.org. |
| Louisiana | *Guide to Vital Statistics Records of Church Archives in Louisiana.* Digitized at FamilySearch.org.<br><br>*Directory of Churches and Religious Organizations in New Orleans.* Digitized at HathiTrust.org. |
| Maine | *Directory of Churches and Religious Organizations in Maine.* Digitized at HathiTrust.org. |
| Maryland | *Guide to Maryland Religious Records* at the Maryland State Archives (http://speccol.mdarchives. state.md.us/pages/churches/index.aspx) is an updated, searchable version of the WPA church records surveys (originals at the archive). |
| Massachusetts | *An Inventory of the Universalist Archives in Massachusetts.* Digitized at HathiTrust.org. *A Description of Manuscript Collections in the Massachusetts Diocesan Library* (Protestant Episcopal Church).<br><br>*Massachusetts black historical records survey files, 1936–1942* (includes African-American churches). Massachusetts State Archives. |
| Michigan | *Directory of churches and religious organizations: Greater Detroit.* Digitized at HathiTrust.org.<br><br>*Inventory of the Church Archives of Michigan* for several denominations and locales. Digitized at HathiTrust.org.<br><br>*Vital Statistics Holdings of Church Archives of Michigan,* Wayne County. Digitized at HathiTrust.org. |
| Minnesota | *Guide to Church Vital Statistics Records in Minnesota: Baptisms, Marriages, Funerals.* Digitized at FamilySearch.org.<br><br>*Directory of Churches and Religious Organizations in Minnesota.* Digitized at HathiTrust.org. |
| Mississippi | *Guide to Vital Statistics in Mississippi: Vol. 2, Church Archives.*<br><br>*Inventory of the Church Archives of Mississippi.* Limited access at HathiTrust.org. |
| Missouri | *Inventory of the Church Archives of Missouri.*<br><br>*Guide to Vital Statistics, Church Records in Missouri.* Limited access at HathiTrust.org. |
| Montana | *Directory of Churches and Religious Organizations in Montana.* Digitized at HathiTrust.org.<br><br>*Inventory of Vital Statistics Records of Churches and Religious Organizations in Montana,* searchable at Ancestry.com (subscription required).<br><br>Finding aid for original manuscript collections (Montana State University) details both projects: http://www.lib.montana.edu/archives/collections/2336.html. |

**Resources by state (*continued*)**

| | |
|---|---|
| **Nebraska** | WPA church records inventories may have been done but final projects have not yet been located. However, History Nebraska hosts a webpage detailing its manuscript church record collections: https://history.nebraska.gov/collections/church-records. |
| **Nevada** | *Inventory of the Church Archives of Nevada,* Roman Catholic, Protestant Episcopal, and perhaps others. Protestant Episcopal volume searchable (snippet view) at Google Books. |
| **New Hampshire** | *Inventory of the Church Archives of New Hampshire.*<br><br>*Guide to Church Vital Statistics Records in New Hampshire.* Digitized at HathiTrust.org.<br><br>*Inventory of the Roman Catholic Church Records in New Hampshire.* Digitized at FamilySearch. org and HathiTrust.org (limited search). |
| **New Jersey** | *Directory of Churches in New Jersey,* various denominations. Searchable at Ancestry.com (subscription required). In Multistate collection, above.<br><br>*Inventory of the Church Archives of New Jersey,* various volumes. Digitized at HathiTrust. org (limited search); searchable at Ancestry.com.<br><br>*Transcriptions of Early Church Records of New Jersey.* Digitized at HathiTrust.org. |
| **New Mexico** | *Directory of Churches and Religious Organizations in New Mexico.* Digitized at HathiTrust.org. |
| **New York** | *Inventory of the Church Archives of New York City* (various denominations). Religious Society of Friends (Quakers), digitized at HathiTrust.org, as is Presbyterian Church in the USA (limited search). *Inventory of the Church Archives of New York State Exclusive of New York City.* Digitized at HathiTrust.org and FamilySearch.org.<br><br>*Inventory of the Church Records of the Protestant Episcopal Church in the Diocese of Western New York.* Digitized at HathiTrust.org.<br><br>Inventories in eLibrary of New York Genealogical & Biographical Society website (https://www.newyorkfamilyhistory.org/); member-only access at press time but expected to be released to public. |
| **North Carolina** | *Inventory of the Church Archives of North Carolina,* various volumes. Limited search at HathiTrust.org. Baptist associations, digitized at HathiTrust.org. |
| **North Dakota** | *Guide to Church Vital Statistics Records in North Dakota.* In Multistate collection, above.<br><br>*North Dakota Church Index.* State Historical Society of North Dakota Archives. |
| **Ohio** | *Inventory of the Church Archives of Ohio Presbyterian Churches.* Original manuscript collection at Ohio History Connection (https://www.ohiohistory.org).<br><br>*Parishes of the Catholic Church Diocese of Cleveland: History and Records* (Cleveland, Ohio: Cadillac Press, 1942).<br><br>*A Preliminary Bibliography Relating to Churches in West Virginia, Virginia, Kentucky, and southern Ohio.* Digitized at HathiTrust.org. |
| **Oklahoma** | *Preliminary List of Churches and Religious Organizations in Oklahoma.* Digitized at HathiTrust.org. *Inventory of the Church Archives of Oklahoma.* Digitized at Archive.org. |
| **Oregon** | *Directory of Churches and Religious Organizations, State of Oregon.* Digitized at HathiTrust. org. |
| **Pennsylvania** | "WPA Church Archives," searchable on Ancestry.com (subscription required). *Inventory of Church Archives, Society of Friends in Pennsylvania.* Digitized at HathiTrust.org. |
| **Rhode Island** | *Directory of Churches and Religious Organizations of Rhode Island.* Digitized at HathiTrust. org. *Guide to Church Vital Statistics Records of Rhode Island.* Digitized at FamilySearch. org. *Inventory of the Church Archives of Rhode Island,* various denominations. Digitized at HathiTrust.org. |

**Resources by state (*continued*)**

| | |
|---|---|
| **South Carolina** | Inventory of South Carolina Church Archives searchable at https://digital.library. sc.edu/collections/inventory-of-s-c-church-archives/. |
| **South Dakota** | None found. |
| **Tennessee** | *Inventory of the Church Archives of Tennessee.* Digitized at Explore KY (https://exploreuk. uky.edu/catalog/xt7jq23qz72t_1#page/1/mode/1up). |
| | *Guide to Church Vital Statistics in Tennessee.* Digitized at HathiTrust.org. *Directory of Churches, Missions and Religious Institutions of Tennessee,* various volumes. Additional collections in Multistate collection, above. |
| **Texas** | Manuscript originals of church archives inventories at the University of Texas at Austin (https://legacy.lib.utexas.edu/taro/utcah/01355/cah-01355.html). |
| **Utah** | *Directory of Churches and Religious Organizations in Utah* (not including The Church of Jesus Christ of Latter-day Saints). Digitized at the Digital Public Library of America (dp.la). |
| | *Inventory of the Church Archives of Utah and Directory of Churches and Religious Organizations in Utah.* Both digitized at HathiTrust.org |
| **Vermont** | *Directory of Churches and Religious Organizations in the State of Vermont* and *Inventory of the Church Archives of Vermont.* Both digitized at HathiTrust.org. |
| **Virginia** | *Inventory of the Church Archives of Virginia.* Also: *Guide to the Manuscript Collections of the Virginia Baptist Historical Society, supplement.* |
| | *A Preliminary Bibliography Relating to Churches in West Virginia, Virginia, Kentucky, and Southern Ohio.* Digitized at HathiTrust.org. |
| **Washington** | *Guide to Church Vital Statistics Records in Washington,* digitized at FamilySearch.org. |
| **Washington, D.C.** | *A Directory of Churches and Religious Organizations in the District of Columbia.* Digitized at HathiTrust.org. |
| **West Virginia** | *Inventory of the Church Archives of West Virginia.* Presbyterian and Protestant Episcopal surveys in Multistate collection, above. |
| | *A Preliminary Bibliography Relating to Churches in West Virginia, Virginia, Kentucky, and southern Ohio.* Digitized at HathiTrust.org. |
| **Wisconsin** | *Directory of Churches and Religious Organizations in Wisconsin.* Digitized at HathiTrust.org and Digital Public Library of America (dp.la). |
| | *Inventory of the Church Archives of Wisconsin,* various volumes. For description of church records projects, Chester W. Bowie, "The Wisconsin Historical Records Survey, Then and Now," *The American Archivist* (April 1974), 247–61, digitized at https:// americanarchivist. org/doi/abs/10.17723/aarc.37.2.n48v4748603g484k. |
| **Wyoming** | *A Directory of Churches and Religious Organizations in the State of Wyoming.* Digitized at HathiTrust.org and the Digital Public Library of America (dp.la). |
| | *Inventory of the Church Archives of Wyoming Presbyterian Churches.*<br>*Guide to Vital Statistics Records in Wyoming: Church Archives.* |

Here are some additional tips and online resources for accessing WPA church record inventories:

- Copies of many are available at the Family History Library in Salt Lake City, Utah, and other major genealogy libraries.
- Search for the name of the state, the phrase "Historical Records Survey," and "church" in WorldCat, Google Books (https://books.google.com), Internet Archive (https://archive. org) and the HathiTrust Digital Archive (https://www.hathitrust.org). Sample search: "Nevada Historical Records Survey church."

- Consult *The WPA Historical Records Survey: A Guide to the Unpublished Inventories, Indexes and Transcripts,*[7] compiled by Loretta L. Hefner.
- Consult "Guide: WPA Related Resources Avaiable at IUB Wells Library," https://libraries. indiana.edu/guide-wpa-related-resources-available-iub-wells-library#HRS.

## At-a-Glance: Where to Search for Church Records in Different Formats

| Format | First try... | Then try | Other search options |
|---|---|---|---|
| Original church records | Local church office, if it still exists | A regional or central denominational archive | WorldCat, ArchiveGrid, NUCMC; state libraries, archives, and historical and genealogical societies |
| Online images, transcriptions, or indexes | Denominational chapters for online records or collections | A general online search for the name of the church, location, and the phrase "membership records" (or similar phrase) | Individual genealogy websites (Ancestry, FamilySearch, Findmypast) and genealogy websites for specific locales or churches |
| Microfilmed images | WorldCat | FamilySearch (search by location) | |
| Published transcriptions in books | WorldCat | Online digital archives: Google Books, Internet Archive, Digital Public Library of America, HathiTrust | FamilySearch (search by location, then record type) |
| Published transcriptions in journal articles | PERiodical Source Index (PERSI) database (free) at Findmypast to identify articles in specific journals | WorldCat to locate nearby copies of the journal | Allen County Public Library Genealogy Center Article Fulfillment service to order copies |

## HELP! WHAT CHURCH IS THIS NOW?

Most churches in the United States have tangled family trees of their own. Consider one example: Presbyterianism. In the denominational tree shown on the next page (courtesy of the Presbyterian Historical Society, Philadelphia, Pennsylvania[8]), a few different initial Presbyterian groups beginning in the United States evolved into at least a dozen strands over the years, which are now represented by at least nine different Presbyterian church associations today.

Denominational trees like these provide fantastic at-a-glance references for anyone trying to trace a particular church forward in history, so you know which archive to contact and what to ask for. A good source for denominational trees is the Association of Religion Data Archives (ARDA), http://www.thearda.com/denoms/families/trees/. Archivists and websites for major religious archives can also help steer you in the right direction.

Histories of religion in the United States can give you more in-depth background on your fam-

7   Loretta L. Hefner, *The WPA Historical Records Survey: A Guide to the Unpublished Inventories, Indexes, and Transcripts* (Chicago: Society of American Archivists, 1980). Later published in *The Midwestern Archivist* 7, no. 1 (1982): 57–59, and at JSTOR (https://www.jstor.org).
8   David Staniunas, *Presbyterian Family Connections* chart; Presbyterian Historical Society (https://www.history.pcusa.org/history-online/presbyterian-history/family-tree-presbyterian-denominations); image permission at https://commons.wikimedia.org/wiki/File:Presbyterian_Family_Connections.jpg.

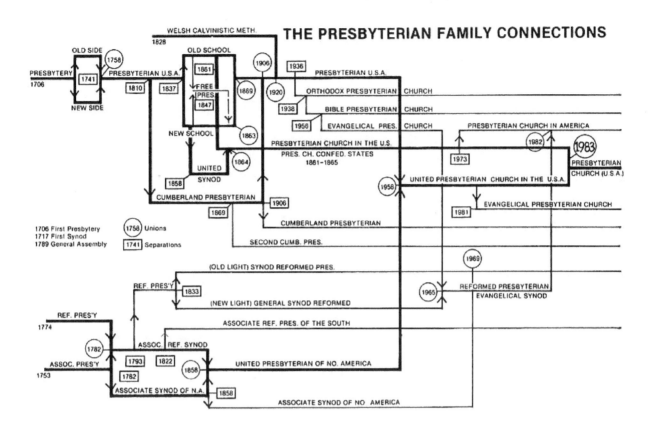

ily's faith (just beware of information overload!). Examples include *Handbook of Denominations in the United States*[9] and *Encyclopedia of American Religions*.[10] Wonderfully thorough but not for the faint of heart is *America's God*.[11] Some states have their own weighty tomes—for example, *Hoosier Faiths*.[12] Denominational histories can be especially helpful when you are trying to trace a congregation's history forward in time. Look for these on WorldCat or at your local library.

Finally, be aware that "union churches" are common in U.S. history. This happened when spiritually like-minded congregations in a town shared their resources: a building, pastoring duties, finances, and—most relevant to you—records. Often you'll see them uniting for a period of years, then going their separate ways due to changes in membership, pastors, or cultures.

Lutheran and Reformed congregations often had union churches, as did many Presbyterian and Congregationalist churches in the early 1800s (there was a formal agreement between the faiths). Published records today will often refer to both congregations in the title, but not always with their full names. If you're looking for records of one of the above churches, also look for records of the other. They might be hidden in plain sight!

9   Craig D. Atwood, Frank S. Mead, and Samuel S. Hill, *Handbook of Denominations in the United States*, 13th ed. (Nashville: Abingdon Press, 2013).
10  John Gordon Melton, *Encyclopedia of American Religions* (Detroit: Gale Research, 2003).
11  Mark A. Noll, *America's God: From Jonathan Edwards to Abraham Lincoln* (New York: Oxford University Press, 2002).
12  L. C. Rudolph, *Hoosier Faiths: A History of Indiana's Churches and Religious Groups* (Bloomington: Indiana University Press, 1995).

*Chapter 4*

# TIPS FOR WORKING WITH OLD CHURCH RECORDS

Having gone to so much trouble to find old church records, you still need to avoid treating them as gospel. You need to cast a skeptical eye on indexes, transcripts, abstracts, microfilm, digital images, and manuscript originals—in order to know what you have and how far these valuable records can be trusted.

## FINDING ORIGINAL RECORDS

### How to trace record copies and indexes to their source

Original records are usually the best for several reasons:

1. They were recorded near the time of the event and sometimes by an eyewitness. (Have you ever compared a postcard from 1960 describing a family escapade to a recollection of it in 2010?)

2. Digital or microfilmed versions may be missing pages or contain images that are cut off or out of focus. And usually just the meatiest genealogical parts of church records (member and rite lists) are imaged, while your family may be mentioned in other places in that church's paperwork (see Chapter 5).

3. Both published and unpublished transcriptions, abstracts, and indexes may contain simple copying errors or omit odd or revealing pieces of information that didn't fit; sometimes they don't even identify the original from which they came.

How can you get to original records from whatever derivative source you may be consulting? Online records of all kinds should include a citation naming the original records, including the record custodian at the time they were imaged or filmed. For example, look at the entry on the next page from the FamilySearch Catalog (at https://familysearch.org) for a Lutheran church in Michigan. In the notes section, it says "Microfilm of originals at the Concordia Historical Institute in St. Louis, Missouri."

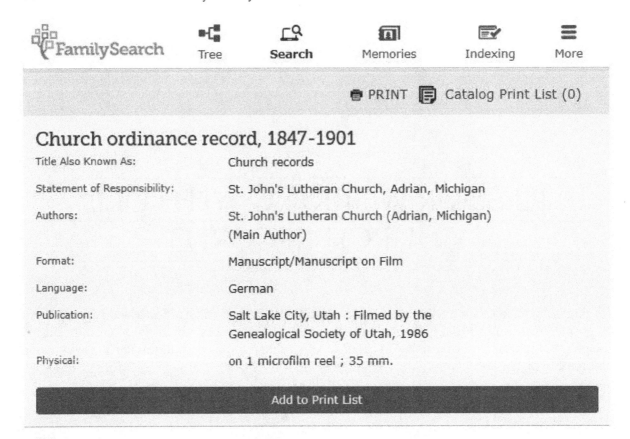

**Notes**
Microfilm of originals at the Concordia Historical Institute in St. Louis, Missouri.

Text in German.

Record contains church constitution; feast days, 1882-1901; family register; baptisms; marriages, 1847-1858; deaths, 1849-1858; confirmations, 1852-1858.

Church records published at most websites also include source citation information. For example, if you're looking at an individual indexed entry in Ancestry's Dutch Reformed Church records collection, you'll see a section called "Source Information" at the bottom of the entry. It reads, "Original data: Dutch Reformed Church Records from New York and New Jersey. Holland Society of New York, New York, New York." That's where to start looking for the original records, if they are needed.

Unfortunately, some online record sets contain no such specific information. If this proves to be the case, try contacting the company, organization, or individual who runs the site and ask where and when they obtained the records and how you can access the originals. Even if you can't learn anything more about them, those online record sets may still provide useful clues, but try not to rely on them excessively.

In published (and sometimes unpublished) record transcripts, you will often find notes about the original sources used and their locations. Here's an example from the beginning of a published transcription of Anglican and Episcopalian records: "This transcription of the parish registers of St. Paul's Parish was taken from the first three volumes of the original registers, which until recently have not been available to researchers. They are found in manuscript collection MS 1727 at the Maryland Historical Society, which spans the years 1710–1924, and fills twelve boxes."[1]

You may also find notes about the condition or accessibility of the original records, such as this statement from a published version of Catholic cemetery records: "The very early records were in poor condition and extreme care was taken to copy accurately. Those from 1863–1915 were in old German script with some Latin spellings. Many pages had disintegrated and fallen into pieces. Some were not in chronological order, making it necessary often to make an educated guess as to the year. . . . Many tombstones were broken and others illegible. Much care was taken to read accurately."[2]

These notations are significant. They show that the compilers did not take things for granted and understood that in transcribing they were making difficult choices or faced uncertainty. Conversely, transcribed records that lack this kind of information, or that only name someone as "typist," may not have been as thoughtfully produced.

All that said, occasionally original records were destroyed or the church does not make them available to researchers. Knowing this helps you understand when you've reached "the end of the road" as far as a path back to original records. Of course, it's always worth double-checking with the local congregation or a church archive. There may still be records of some kind available.

When originals are not available, digital or microfilmed versions come closest and are often a good substitute. Watch for signs that an imaging job was done well, with quality images that include the entire page (no sign of omissions or alterations or inconsistencies) and source information. Any version (be it an image copy or a transcript) that's illegible, lacks source information, has rearranged or missing pages, or merely copies an earlier derivative version isn't as reliable. Either continue to search for original records or obtain a more responsible derivative version, or explain why your findings may be incomplete or inaccurate.

## WHAT TO LOOK FOR IN THE RECORDS

### Check for instructions followed by the clerks

Even originals have their secrets. Don't gallop through looking for your names. Start at the beginning. Preprinted membership registers, for instance, often have a page of instructions at the beginning (less common in entirely handwritten records). On page 40 is an example of the instructions printed in the beginning of an Episcopalian membership register.[3]

These instructions can act like a secret decoder ring. They may describe abbreviations used, the meaning of different types of entries, etc. One good test of a published transcript: If it's good, it includes a full copy of the original instructions. Of course, those who filled in membership registers may not have always followed the instructions, but reading them can still help.

### Study the handwriting

Sometimes it takes time and effort and immersion to decipher old handwriting. Read several entries by the same hand. The ones that are easy to read can help identify—letter by letter if needed—sloppier or less obvious ones. Similarly, read down a column to better understand what's written there. If you need more help, search online with the phrase "handwriting help for genealogists" (add a foreign language keyword as needed). Several excellent online resources are available.

---

1   Robert Barnes, "Introduction," *Records of St. Paul's Parish* (Westminster, Md.: Family Line Publications, 1988).

2   "Acknowledgments," *St. Bernard's Catholic Church, Akron, Ohio Cemetery Inscriptions and Funeral Records* (Akron, Ohio: Summit County Chapter Ohio Genealogical Society, 1991).

3   "How to Use This Book," *Trinity Episcopal Church Registers, Fort Wayne, Indiana*, Vol. 2, 1889–1923, n.p. [front matter].

# HOW TO USE THIS BOOK.

---

**T**HE following suggestions and explanations may be of service to clergymen.

## I.—FAMILIES.

1. Arrange them in the order in which each family became connected with the parish.
2. Give to each family, less than twelve in number, the space *across the page* between the horizontal red lines; thus keeping each family distinct, and leaving room to note subsequent changes. If the family contains twelve or more names, combine two of the horizontal spaces.
3. Write the *ordinal number* I, II, III, IV, etc., under the heading "Number," on the intersection of the double red lines.
4. Insert the maiden name of the wife. Place the names of *children* immediately after those of parents, and other names always in the second column.
5. The *age* recorded should correspond to the date in the first column.
6. The heading, *B. C. C.*, indicates the abbreviations used respectively for those *baptized, confirmed or communicants.*
7. *Deaths* may be indicated by the mark (\*) immediately before the names; *removals* by the mark (†).
8. A list of families thus kept *will not need re-writing* while the register lasts.

## II.—BAPTISMS.

1. *Day and Date.* That is, *ecclesiastical* and *civil* date.
2. *Place.* If not in Church, state at what house.
3. In recording *adult* baptisms, write "adult" under the surname.
4. Give the family name of the mother, the residence of the parents, and the residence and relationship to the child of sponsors other than parents.
5. Every baptism should be authenticated, if possible, by the *signature* of the clergyman officiating.
6. *Certifications* of Private Baptisms, which were not performed in the parish, may be noted on the last line of the page; other certifications, under the "Day and Date," and "Place" of the Private Baptism.

## III.—CONFIRMED.

1. Give names in *full.* Note the *place,* if other than the Church.
2. *Baptism.* If in the parish, a reference (by number or page) to entries of baptisms is sufficient; if elsewhere, give the name of the parish or religious body in which it was performed.

## IV.—COMMUNICANTS.

1. "*Day and Date*"—of reception, or first Communion *in the parish.*
2. "Number"—as in all cases refers to the chronological order in which the names and date should be written.
3. Write the *year* distinctly above the names added for that year, leaving a blank line above and below it.
4. The narrow column immediately before the name is intended to show at a glance the deaths (\*), removals (†), and suspensions or withdrawals (‡).
5. Write the maiden name of married women in a parenthesis *before* the surname; the surname added by marriage after becoming a communicant, in a parenthesis *after* the maiden name: e. g., *Mrs. A— (B—) C—; Miss A— B— (C—).* A representing the Christian name, B the maiden name, C the husband's name.
6. *C. A. R.* Denoted by *C,* those *admitted* to communion on their confirmation in the parish; *A,* those *admitted* otherwise, adding *C,* if subsequently *confirmed; R,* those *received* from another parish. In the latter case, give the name of the parish "whence received."
7. The name of the communicant returning after removal should, as a general rule, be re-entered at the foot of the list. Except in such cases, no name need be recorded more than once. If the removal is temporary or uncertain, the mark (†) may be in pencil, and thus easily erased.

## V.—MARRIAGES.

1. "*Place*" i. e. in Church; or at what house.
2. The names and *residence* of two or more special witnesses should be recorded.

## VI.—BURIALS.

1. After the name of a wife, note that of her husband; after that of a child, those of its parents, &c.

## VII.—INDEX.

It may often be found convenient to arrange the INDEX in the form of an *Index Rerum,* by dividing the space given to each initial into five subdivisions, heading each with an initial and vowel, the latter representing the first vowel of the name, as Aa, Ae, Ai, Ao, Auy, &c. The proportions of the vowels under different initials may be readily found by looking through any alphabetical list—as the Clergy List in the Church Almanac—or, still better, by first preparing a list from the Parish Records, and regulating the spaces accordingly.

ADVENT, 1859.

You can also crowdsource your puzzle. Facebook has thousands of genealogy groups centered around certain locales, languages, ethnic origins, and the like. In your Facebook search box, enter the word "genealogy" along with the language or place to see what groups exist. Some are more active than others, and the quality of responses varies. You may need to shop your question across a few different groups in order to find helpful answers. The Transitional Genealogists Forum is an open email list at https://mailinglists.rootsweb.com/listindexes/. Also, consider joining the Association of Professional Genealogists, which maintains a members-only email list (more at https://www.apgen.org). Helpful people at all skill levels lurk there.

Handwriting patterns can help you understand whether you are looking at a list of entries made gradually as time unfolded or whether you are looking at a list that was copied from an earlier one, or was created retrospectively. Why do you care? An entry made at the time of the event is generally more accurate. Similarly, a list created over time is likely more complete than one created years later (how complete a list could you create today of your high-school graduating class?).

For example, see the First Congregational Church membership register image shown on page 7. Many of the names appear to be written in the same handwriting, and perhaps even at the same time, as the ink and cadence of the writing are consistent. The last three entries on the page are written in pencil, as are all the entries in the "Removals" columns and two of the entries in the "Remarks" column. The admittance date for Mrs. Libby Fraser appears initially to have been written as "Dec. 1877," with the day, "25th," perhaps written in later. These observations may provide clues when evaluating the content and trustworthiness of this record.

## Look at your relatives' entries in context

Comparing information about your ancestors with what's written about other church members can help put their lives in context. Were there a lot of deaths during the season your relative died? Were births other than that of your ancestor marked as "ill" or "col" (illegitimate or colored)? Did a lot of mothers or infants die from childbirth at that time?

One compiler of cemetery records noticed patterns in the data, which to him signified a larger theme:

> Going beyond the bald facts of names and dates presented here, in a thoughtful perusal one can read the sad record of the cholera epidemics of 1849, 1850 and 1852, which devastated the city, and the smaller epidemic of 1854. One also becomes aware of how difficult life was, how many children were lost in infancy and childhood, and how many adults died in what is now usually a healthy middle age. On the other hand, one sees hints of kindness: a poor person lovingly buried on another family's lot; the good work of the sisters at St. Francis Hospital; the efforts of the hard-working pastor who was apparently too ill himself to record the deaths during one week of the 1852 epidemic.[4]

Other patterns in the record-keeping may help you better interpret them. For example, in the United Presbyterian and Congregational baptismal record shown on page 6, all the entries on that page included a parent's name. On other pages, however, a few entries instead said "Adult" in the column for parents' names. This introduces the possibility that all baptisms with parents' names were for minors, as appears to have been the practice in some records.

## Look for mention of other family members

Once you've found one relative in a church's records, you're likely to find more. Do you see any of the following?

- Other records for the same person? Remember that there may be birth, baptismal, confirmation, membership admission/dismission, marriage, death, and burial records.

---

4  Donald M. Schlegel, *The Columbus Catholic Cemetery History and Records, 1846–1874* (Columbus, Ohio: Columbus History Service, 1983), iii.

- Other names with the same surname grouped next to your ancestor on a membership list? Or people with other familiar surnames—maternal relatives, in-laws (or future in-laws), cousins, aunts and uncles, etc.? For example, the Congregational membership register on page 7 includes some male-female pairs of the same surname who are listed in sequence with the same admittance date, hinting that they might be married couples.

- Births or marriages of anyone else with the same parents as your ancestor?

- Family names listed as sponsors/godparents, witnesses, or other roles? Sometimes published records include indexes to these names. In many churches, grandparents and other close relatives filled these roles.

- A couple of the same surname baptizing a child on the same day as your ancestors?

Keep in mind that church records may not be entirely in alphabetical or chronological order. Clerks or ministers often added additional notes later on to correct errors or add people whose names were missed. Valuable bits of information may be tacked on at the end of a list, the bottom of a page, or anywhere else the person had room to put them (for example, a Presbyterian record with a separate list of infant deaths at the end of the regular list of deaths). A published record for a German Evangelical Lutheran and German Union church[5] notes that the following appeared "on scraps of paper in record book":

> Sarah Ellen born March 22, 1837
> Mary Jane born February 7, 1840
> John Andrew born August 29, 1841
> Baptized the 1st of Aprile 1841 by David Winters

Then the transcriber included her own guesses on the identity of these children, as no surnames were given.

## GUIDELINES FOR USING THE RECORDS

### Work carefully with original records

Every archive has its own rules on the use of original records. Here are some guidelines you may be asked to follow when visiting an archive, and some additional tips for a good research experience:

- Wash your hands. You may or may not be asked to wear white archival gloves.

- Use only pencil to write down your own notes. (You may or may not be allowed to use your laptop.) Never mark the original record or even run your pencil lightly over it. Don't write on paper that is sitting on top of original documents. Don't add clips or sticky notes and don't fold over the page corners. If you need to mark a page, use an approved bookmark.

- Opening an old book or ledger all the way may stress the spine. Additionally, the pages may not lie flat. Don't overstress the book spine or push the pages. Request a book cradle, which will hold the book in a mostly open position and may help pages to lie flatter. Turn pages gently.

- Handle all loose documents gently. Torn or fragile papers may need to be lifted with both hands.

- If you come across unusual record damage or deterioration (especially if an archivist may not know about it), report it to a staff member at the archive.

- Leave items in the order in which you find them. While it may make sense to you to reorder them, there was likely a reason for the original order.

---

5  Carleen Olds Roe, compiler and indexer, *Church Records of Beaver United Church of Christ, Beavercreek Twp., Greene County, Ohio: In 1824 The German Evangelic Lutheran and German Union Church* (privately published, 1974), 9.

- Don't take anything, even a small scrap of paper—even if it has your ancestor's name or handwritten signature on it. Stealing archival material is a crime and will likely be prosecuted.

- Ask permission before taking digital images or scans—but take them if you can! Do not press a handheld imaging device directly onto original pages without permission.

- Request photocopies too—both color (because various inks or marks may show up better) and black and white (because they will last longer).

- Once you've confirmed your family's participation in a church, look beyond the membership records to any financial, administrative, or ministerial materials in that collection. (Learn more about these records in Chapter 5.)

### Get the most out of published records

Published and unpublished transcripts of records have some clear disadvantages: things may be left out, transcribed incorrectly, or otherwise changed from the original. Wherever possible, try to get back to the original records. But don't ignore transcripts. Why?

1. They may be all that is available to researchers due to the loss of the original, protection of fragile records, or confidentiality.

2. They are often findable through online catalogs like WorldCat and available through interlibrary loan. Original records are less easy to find and not borrowable.

3. They are usually much more easily read than the originals and are often indexed. A few have every-name indexes—not just to those baptized, for example, but also to the names of sponsors and parents.

As indicated earlier, transcripts often contain explanatory notes and even supplementary research not included in the original. These descriptions not only tell you what you're looking at, they also hint at how experienced and careful the transcribers were. This is helpful if you find conflicting data elsewhere: you'll need to weigh how reliable the information is likely to be in each case.

Finally, sometimes published records contain fantastic (in both senses) supplementary information. Most commonly, you'll find a brief history of the church, photographs of its buildings, and similar background. The following description of the First German Protestant Cemetery of Avondale, Ohio, is priceless, the more so because the cemetery itself doesn't exist anymore:

> It had a large iron gate entrance at 2632 Reading Road over which hung a key. Legend often repeated that anyone who touched the key would die within the year. It became known as the cholera cemetery by 1878. People feared even digging the ground where cholera victims had been placed. It was closed in 1878. . . . As time passed, the cemetery was forgotten. In 1966, the cemetery grounds were sold to the Cincinnati Board of Education, then covered over with black asphalt for a school playground. Today, no visible trace remains of the original cemetery.[6]

Occasionally, the transcriber includes additional research on the people in the records. The preface to one such book reads:

> By using research already done by others, I was able to write up fairly complete biographical sketches of a majority of the pew holders and vestrymen mentioned in the old documents. The obituaries [in microfilmed newspapers] often told when and where in New England the person was born, his parents' names and his wife's maiden name. The censuses listed his children, and the obituary told whom the daughters had married and where the various children had settled.[7]

---

6  Jeffery Herbert, ed., *Hamilton County, Ohio Burial Records*, Vol. 13: [Translations of], *First German Protestant Cemetery of Avondale & Martini United Church of Christ Records* (2001; Berwyn Heights, Md.: Heritage Books, 2009), i.

7  Mary Anne Denison Cummins, *St Peter's Episcopal Church, Delaware, Ohio: The First Hundred Years 1817–1918; A Collection of Documents and Genealogical Data* (Westminster, Md.: Heritage Books, 2010), vii.

Another transcriber, Margaret Bouic, did something similar in *Ostrander Presbyterian Church and Its Members*.[8] She supplemented church registers with data from local government records and even interviews with relatives.

These gifts are well-intended but can be a mixed blessing. Some transcribers fail to distinguish between the information in the original record and the results of their own research, greatly diminishing the value of the transcription. Some refer casually to research done by "others," without evaluating its quality. And some who do distinguish their own conclusions from the original records fail to cite their sources, which at least is a failure that can usually be remedied. Treat this additional information as hints to be verified independently.

---

8   Margaret Main Bouic, *Ostrander Presbyterian Church and Its Members* (Ostrander, Ohio: privately published, 1962).

*Chapter 5*

# MORE RECORDS ABOUT CHURCH LIFE

In addition to keeping records on individual church members, churches created other records describing the lives of their members. After you have confirmed an ancestor's membership in a church, it's sometimes worth looking for

- congregational histories;
- denominational histories and encyclopedias;
- church newspapers;
- original (generally unpublished) administrative records including
  - creeds, by-laws, and rules of conduct,
  - donor or subscriber lists,
  - Sunday School attendance records,
  - minutes of meetings,
  - pew rental lists,
  - correspondence,
  - church auxiliary and association records;
- ministers' private records; and
- church cemetery records.

The first three types of records are published and therefore usually easier to find. The fourth type includes many smaller items, often all found together in manuscript collections. The last two items on the list—ministers' records and cemetery records—are rarely published and are often found separate from other original church records.

## PARISH AND CONGREGATIONAL HISTORIES

Many churches celebrate important anniversaries by having their histories written. At the outset of one such history, a minister writes:

> This little pamphlet will contain various interesting statistics—vital, social and financial—which will very exactly describe the condition under which this parish is organized. . . . We are living in a country where everything, men and things are constantly changing and shifting. What may not interest us much, at the present date, will form very curious and instructive reading for our children and grandchildren in a generation or two, when the stone and brick we bought for their religious comfort may still look as bright as they look today, but when "we" shall certainly be no more.[1]

---

1   Rev. P. H. Steyle, "Introduction," *Memorial Record of St. Mary's Parish, Delaware, Ohio, January 1911–January 1986* (Columbus, Ohio: C. G. Gray, 1986).

Congregational histories often include the following:

- When the congregation was organized and by whom
- Where it has met over the years
- Names of ministers, pastors, and others who presided or officiated
- Names and contributions (spiritual, social, or financial) of prominent members
- Descriptions of schools, auxiliaries, and other organizations sponsored by the church
- Offshoot congregations of the same faith or "competing" faiths in the same geographic area
- Photos of members, church buildings, social events, First Communion classes, etc.

Some parish or congregational histories even contain transcribed records of selected early church records, such as a charter membership list, roster of pastors, or early baptisms. Finding even *some* records mentioned in a church history tells you that those records exist (or did at one time). Use whatever clues are provided to track them down.

Church histories are usually printed in quantity even when not formally published, so it's generally possible to find copies. Ask at the congregational office (if it still exists), a regional or central church archive, local historical and genealogical societies, and/or the local public library (especially its local history department).

It's also worth searching online in all the places you'd usually look for genealogical and historical records:

- WorldCat (search the catalog for the name and location of the church)
- A separate keyword search for the name and location of the church (consider adding the word "history"), which may bring up digitized versions or entries in online library catalogs
- Online catalogs of regional, denominational, university, historical, and religious libraries and archives, whose results may not be picked up by your search engine

For example, a Google search for the terms "history Methodist Linn Creek Missouri" brings up a PDF-format finding aid for an item at the State Historical Society of Missouri. The item is called "The History of 90 Years of Linn Creek Methodist Church, from 1874 to 1964," compiled by Mrs. F. L. Ridenour. To access the item, you would contact the State Historical Society of Missouri to confirm whether it's available to researchers in person (if you can go there) or remotely (by ordering a copy).

Though this 1964 booklet was most likely a printed item, it's considered rare enough that it's part of an archival collection now. Its finding aid is particularly useful because it summarizes the history of *two* Methodist congregations in that town.

## DENOMINATIONAL HISTORIES AND ENCYCLOPEDIAS

Most U.S. religions have had several books written about their origins and history, settlement patterns, ethnic makeup, doctrine, policies, social history, and more. Regional histories, such as a history of Catholicism in Maryland or Methodism in the antebellum South, may be especially enlightening—so may books published by church authorities or scholars.

To find books like these, use the same research tools already outlined in this book for finding other published materials. Search for keywords like "Catholic history Maryland" in WorldCat or the catalog of your favorite research library. Click on a promising title to see its subject headings and browse related titles.

Here's an example of how a passage from a church history or manual can help you understand the records. Let's say you read that your ancestor was censured by her Congregationalist church in the mid-1800s. What did that mean? Was she cut off from the church? What did that involve? You can find an answer in an 1867 book (found on Google Books with the search terms "Congregational church history censures excommunication"):

> The exercise of discipline is not delegated to one or more individuals in the church, whether officers or otherwise. The duty rests upon the whole church. Its purpose is the purification of the church, and the reclaiming of offenders. . . . A brother goes alone to the offender. Failing to obtain Christian satisfaction he takes another with him. Failing still, he tells it to the church, presenting charges in due form with proper specifications, and naming witnesses by whose testimony they are to be sustained. The church must then furnish the accused with a copy of the charges and the names of witnesses. . . . The Censures of the church are Admonition, Suspension, and Excommunication or withdrawal of Fellowship. Admonition has no effect upon the church privileges or the admonished, and may or may not be followed by further disciplinary action at the discretion of the church. Suspension cuts off from all the privileges of the church, and if the offender is not reclaimed, must be followed by excommunication. Excommunication is the last resort, to be adopted only after kind and patient effort has failed to restore the offender. Congregationalism knows no egress from the church but by death, by letter [dismissal to another church], or by excommunication.[2]

Keep in mind that most every church has supporters and detractors, and both may have written histories that reflect the writer's general prejudices and opinions on the church's beliefs, politics, and social practices. Older history books may be especially biased and less inclusive of women and ethnic minorities.

## CHURCH NEWSPAPERS

Many churches printed regional or national newspapers for their members. These reported church events, appointments of ministers or teachers at church schools, preaching schedules, and more. They also reported marriages and deaths, not just of ministers but of everyday members like this twenty-four-year-old woman whose obituary ran in an 1844 edition of the Methodist *Western Christian Advocate*.[3]

> ELEANOR REED, daughter of Robert and Jane Fielding, and late consort of Robert Reed, was born in Cumberland county, Pa. She was converted to God at a camp meeting held at Poplar Grove for Connersville circuit, in the year 1834, and immediately applied for membership in the Methodist Episcopal Church. In October, 1841, she was married to Mr. Robert Reed, and with her husband removed to Delaware county, Ia., where she departed this life on the 19th of February, 1844, in the 24th year of her age. She was a Christian in truth and indeed, and her death was tranquil and happy.
> W. W. HIBBEN.

Religious newspapers were popular during the mid-to-late 1800s. Baptist and Methodist papers were especially numerous, but other faiths had them too. Many individual Catholic dioceses published their own papers. The Dutch Reformed Church published *Christian Intelligencer* from 1888 to 1894, which included marriage and death notices.

There are several ways to determine whether a church had a newspaper that covered your ancestor's region at the time. The simplest is to ask the church archivist for that denomination in that region or diocese. You'll likely get both a knowledgeable answer and information about where to access the paper (possibly at that very archive). Other options include librarians or archivists at religious universities and seminaries.

2  Darius E. Jones, ed., *Songs for the New Life Designed for Public, Social and Private Christian Uses* (Cincinnati: John Church Co., 1897), 266.
3  W. W. Hibben, "Eleanor Reed" (obituary), *Western Christian Advocate*, Fri. 28 June 1844, p. 44, col. 2.

Many church newspapers didn't have long runs, but they don't need to have been in print during every year of an ancestor's life to include his or her name. Prioritize your search for newspapers published around the time a family member died or married.

Once you've identified a denominational newspaper, look for an index by asking in person at a repository or searching online. Search WorldCat for the title of the newspaper or for associated keywords (like "Methodist and Missouri") for print indexes, or consult *Obituaries: A Guide to Sources*.[4] Don't forget to search PERSI (see Chapter 3) for articles in genealogical publications. If you've found a knowledgeable archivist or librarian, you can also ask about existing indexes.

As an alternative, or if there is no published index, search out a digitized, microfilmed, or print copy of the newspaper. A good website with links to thousands of online newspaper resources is The Ancestor Hunt (http://www.theancestorhunt.com/newspaper-research-links.html). Many religious newspapers have been digitized on the Library of Congress's Chronicling America webpage (https://chroniclingamerica.loc.gov/).

Also use Chronicling America to find original and microfilmed copies in libraries. Click on "US Newspaper Directory, 1690–Present." Then search for the name of the newspaper. You may see multiple entries with title variations and different years, as well as the name of a city in parentheses—this is the city from which the paper was published, not necessarily the entire geographic area of interest for the paper. Click on an entry that looks likely, then click on "Holdings" to see a list of libraries that have it. Contact the library to see if they will lend it through interlibrary loan.

## ORIGINAL ADMINISTRATIVE PAPERS

The original administrative records of a local congregation do not always survive, and they are almost never indexed. Not every researcher will think it worth the effort to pursue these records. But the most diligent, determined, and/or desperate ones will. If extant, the records may reveal fascinating facts that you can't learn anywhere else. Three approaches to finding these are as follows:

- If you've found the membership records still at the church, ask the congregational office about the old administrative records and whether they are now in an archive.
- If you've found the membership records at an archive, check the description of the manuscript collection to see if the administrative records are with them.
- If you've found transcribed, microfilmed, or digitized membership records, look at the source citation information for the originals. Chances are good the administrative records were not imaged, but they may be with the membership records, as mentioned above.

Often, a church's earliest records were all kept in a single self-contained volume. Once a church was better established, and after pre-printed volumes became available in the late 1800s, different record types may have had their own separate books.

You may find the following among these documents.

### Creeds, by-laws, and rules of conduct

Many congregations, especially those unaffiliated with other churches, defined their own beliefs and made their own rules. This generally happened when the church was organized.

A creed defines a congregation's core beliefs. A profession of faith is any rote statement to which a new member agrees. Sometimes there is a separate code of conduct or rules and/or rules out-

---

4  Betty M. Jarboe, *Obituaries: A Guide to Sources,* 2nd ed. (Boston: G. K. Hall, 1989).

lining disciplinary measures (which become especially interesting if you find a family member was disciplined by the church). For example, a Congregational church in Ohio in the early 1800s included this statement among its rules: "It is considered by this church that either the sale, furnishing, or habitual use of intoxicating drinks, as a beverage, is inconsistent with the spirit of the Christian profession, and is an offence [sic] deserving church discipline."[5]

These founding documents may include names of the congregation's charter members, those who came together to organize the church. Husbands and wives are often listed together on such a list, which might be separate from any church membership roster.

### Lists of donors or subscribers

Most churches supported ministers, building projects, charitable work, and other ongoing or occasional expenses by asking members for donations. These may have been one-time donations or ongoing subscriptions or pledges (monthly or weekly commitments). You may learn exactly how much money individual members pledged and how well they followed through.

In the records of a Baptist church in Garrettsville, Ohio, created by Elder William West,[6] there's a handwritten, two-column donation list dated January 25, 1812. It mentions over a dozen people who each donated between $2 and $16. That may not sound like much of a genealogical discovery, but that part of Ohio was still sparsely settled. This record might be the only place some church members' names appear in local documents during that time—especially the few women who are listed.

Donations were occasionally for something very specific—and perhaps revealing. For example, in the 1840s, Luther Spelman donated $3 to his local Congregational church, provided that "the chorister will in all cases audibly name the tune before singing and not sing until the choir have learned the tunes named and will allow all to sing that please."[7]

These lists do not generally include dates of birth or family relationships (with the exception of relatives listed together). But they confirm the person's residence and affiliation, and may lead to other relatives.

### Sunday School records

Some churches held religious education classes apart from worship. (The best known of these are Sunday Schools.) The teacher often kept detailed attendance records. An ancestor's attendance confirms his or her residence during that exact time. Sudden absence or withdrawal may signal a family illness, move, or separation from the church. A pattern of absence may indicate your ancestor's participation in harvest season, business travels, or the like.

Minutes of religious education classes may also exist. The Sunday School minutes of a Latter-day Saint congregation in rural Idaho in the 1890s reveal a rare and intimate glimpse of a family's religious life. Over the course of several months, Washington McClellan's name was mentioned regularly as he prayed, made announcements, administered the sacrament (bread and water), provided instruction, and eventually even presided (led the meeting). His wife performed a song at one meeting and his young son gave a recitation.[8]

---

5  "Brecksville Congregational Church Records 1816–1867," p. 11, Record Book 1816–1863; MS 3168, Box 1, Folder 1, Western Reserve Historical Society, Cleveland.

6  "Garrettsville Baptist Church Records, 1808–1860," MS 2087, Box 1, Folder 2, n.p.: Western Reserve Historical Society, Cleveland.

7  "Congregational Church, Wayne, Ashtabula County, Ohio, Records, 1826–1841," MS 1777, Box 1, Folder 1, Western Reserve Historical Society, Cleveland.

8  "Dempsey Ward, Pocatello Stake [later Lava Ward, Portneuf Stake] Sunday School Minutes, 1893–1943," LR 4749 15, Church History Library, The Church of Jesus Christ of Latter-day Saints, Salt Lake City, Utah.

## Minutes of congregational meetings

Minutes record meetings of church leaders and councils. In addition to decisions, actions, and opinions, they may mention baptisms, births, deaths, and move-in or move-out activities of members, even if a separate membership register exists. You may find efforts to resolve conflicts and judgments against members who have misbehaved or neglected church attendance. The latter are especially common among faiths with strict conduct standards, like Quakers and Baptists. Here you may also find financial records such as reports on a building project or a donation list like the one already mentioned for the Garrettsville Baptist Church.

If you already know your family affiliated with a particular church, it's worth reading any surviving minutes for that time period. They're not usually indexed, so it may take some time and patience. Occasionally, you may find reference to church minutes alongside your ancestor's mention in membership records. For example, J. Willis Wolcott was added to the membership list of a Presbyterian-Congregationalist church in 1823, but an "x" next to his name is footnoted at the bottom of the page with the word "Suspended," followed by a subsequent note, "Restored Page 23." If you turn to page 23, you'll find an 1851 entry that reads:

> The case of Br. J.W. Wolcott was called up. Notice was taken of the fact that for some months past, he has regularly attended preaching here with his family, & the members generally expressed their confidence in his Christian character. On motion it was voted that all censure be removed from brother Josiah Willis Wolcott, & that he be invited to participate in all the ordinances & privileges of the church.[9]

Not only does this passage tell a unique story, it also reveals the full name of J. W. Wolcott, which the membership list does not.

Different denominations may have kept minutes in different ways. In the Anglican Church, the comparable record set is the vestry books. Most have not survived, but because they were a semi-governmental record-keeping body, they contain even more information (see the chapter on Anglican records).

## Pew rentals

The practice of renting out pews was common in many churches, in some cases extending into the late 1800s. Records of pew rentals may vary. The published records of Prince George's Chapel in Delaware include a list of the first pew holders in 1758.[10] The list was made by pew number, with multiple families in each pew. Much-later records from a Methodist church in Cleveland[11] included a numbered diagram showing the pew layout, along with names of families who had paid for rights to many of the pews. Extant pew rental records are not common. Look for them with the financial records and/or minutes of the church.

## Correspondence

Among the loose original papers of a church may be original letters of transfer (see an example on page 9) and other correspondence. Here's a poignant letter penned by a grieving widower on January 26, 1901: [12]

---

9 "Record book containing minutes and lists, 1844–1866," United Presbyterian and Congregational Church Records, Farmington Twp., Trumbull Co., Ohio; MS 2125, Folder 2, manuscript page 23, Western Reserve Historical Society, Cleveland.
10 Eugene F. Castrovillo, Jr., *History of Prince George's Chapel, Dagsboro, Delaware* (Dagsboro, Del.: Archaeology Excavation Inc., 1985), n.p.
11 Pew diagram, First Methodist Episcopal Church, Cleveland, Ohio, in "University Circle United Methodist Church Records" [including predecessor churches]; MS 5172, Western Reserve Historical Society, Cleveland, Ohio.
12 John Noble letter 26 Jan. 1901, "Brecksville Congregational Church Records 1816–1867"; MS 3168, Box 2, Folder 4, loose paper, Western Reserve Historical Society, Cleveland.

Dear Sir,

My Dear Wife died this morning at 2 ½ oclock. Can you give the date when she united with the Brecksville Cong[regational] Church. Have you the old records, would be pleased if you are able to give it.

very truly yours, John Noble
Funeral services on Tuesday 11:00 at the house / 12 at the Church at Richfield[?]

### Association participation

Protestant churches that belonged to a larger association or conference likely kept records of that relationship. These records may include annual conference attendance and activities, including lists of local delegates; regular statistical reports of church finances, attendance, or membership; and communications about changes in policy or doctrine and elections of officers.

These records are less likely to mention everyday church members. Consult them when your relative was involved in regional church government or was a minister with varying assignments and locations, or when you are trying to assess the wealth, membership, or other features of the congregation as a whole.

### Auxiliary records

Many churches, especially during the 1800s, included charitable organizations, missionary societies, ladies' auxiliaries, groups to promote temperance or other causes, and the like. There may be separate records of these groups' activities, including membership lists, minutes, financial records, and more. Look for these if you have reason to believe your ancestor may have been involved or if you're having trouble learning more about the women in the family. Women were especially active in religious auxiliaries.

## MINISTERS' RECORDS

Pastors often kept personal records of their ministerial lives. They may have logged all the rites they performed, from baptisms to funerals. They may have listed sermons preached, along with the text and when they were given. They may have kept their correspondence. Traveling ministers often noted the places they visited and preached.

Unfortunately, only a small number of these have been published. The *Pastor's Ideal Vest-Pocket Record and Ritual and Pastor's Ideal Funeral Book* kept by L. F. Miller of Amesville, Ohio, in the early 1900s[13] has now been transcribed and published. There are sections with lists of members' names, funerals preached (including the name and age of the deceased, and the place and the text of the funeral), and sermons preached (with date and place). Another volume, *Bishop [William] White's Private Marriages, 1801–1836,*[14] transcribes the clergyman's personal records of marriages performed. According to the introduction, "Most of these marriages are included among the general marriage records of Christ Church and St. Peter's church. However, some are previously unpublished and many were originally transcribed incorrectly."

Ministers (and those who handled their estates) usually considered these records to be private property. At the minister's death, the records may have been destroyed, lost, kept within the family, or donated to an archive. Before churches began organizing their own central archives in the 1900s, original records of ministers may have ended up in any archive near his final place of

---

13   Scotty L. and Lorine Davis Howard, eds., *Pastor's Ideal Vest-Pocket Record and Ritual and Pastor's Ideal Funeral Book Belonging to L. F. Miller, Amesville, Ohio,* 1916–1950 (Athens, Ohio: Howard Tree, 1984).

14   Harry C. Adams, transcriber, *Bishop [William] White's Private Marriages, 1801–1836* (Doylestown, Penn.: Bucks County Genealogical Society, 2003).

ministry (or wherever the eventual donors lived). However, many records donated in the 20th century have found their way into church archives.

If you know the name of a minister who baptized, married, or buried your relative but can't find the church records, try searching WorldCat and online archival catalogs like ArchiveGrid for that minister's name (see Chapter 3). For the late 1800s and beyond, see whether the denomination kept an annual directory that included ministerial assignments, such as the *Catholic Directory*. Specific denominational chapters later in this book describe records created about the ministers of each faith.

If your relative was a minister, additional records may exist about his ministry. These may include the following:

- His name in a list of pastors kept by a congregation to which he was assigned, along with his name listed as officiant in members' church rites
- Additional biographical or genealogical clues within the historical records or histories of congregations to which he was assigned (especially if he permanently resided there)
- Records of training, ordination, assignments to specific congregations or committees and additional church service, which may have been published in church annuals or at least recorded by a regional or central governing body of the church
- Biographical profiles or memorials published in church newspapers or historical journals
- Minister's biographical or ministerial service files, kept by a central or regional church archive

Some of these records exist for John A. Felix, a United Brethren minister on Sunny Morton's family tree. With the help of staff from the United Brethren Historical Center in Indiana (see the denominational chapter on German Reformed and Sectarian churches), Sunny traced John's affiliation to the branch of the church that eventually merged with the United Methodist Church. She identified the correct annual Methodist conference to which his region eventually belonged; its archive in northwestern Pennsylvania sent her copies of lengthy memorials for John and his wife that appeared in conference journals. Sunny visited the archive and paged through more annual conference journals. These reported annually on his ministerial training, assignments, salary, committees, and fitness for duty. An abstracted pastoral record found on file listed all his ministerial appointments, conference relations, his death date, and the memorial publication information for himself and his spouse.

## CHURCHYARD CEMETERIES

Church burial registers were already discussed in Chapter 2. Though less common, church cemeteries may also have kept maps, details of plot purchases, and lists of all burials in a family plot. Some include stillborn children, who may not have any other birth or death records.

"These records are essential for locating the grave sites and providing information on the individuals buried there," states the Southern Baptist Historical Library and Archives website. "The need to relocate cemeteries or the damage suffered by grave markers makes the survival of these records important to family members and the church. As gravestones deteriorate, an awkward confusion might develop if the written record of cemetery plots is lost. While most cemeteries are well kept, more than a few rural cemeteries have been abandoned. When this happens, the church records may be all that survive."[15]

---

15  Bill Sumners, "Archive Helps: Vital Church Records," Southern Baptist Historical Library and Archives (http://www.sbhla.org/art_vital.htm).

Church cemetery associations' original bylaws or rules can also provide illuminating context. For instance, they may indicate who could and could not be buried there, the cost or dues, and the size of original family plots. The rules of the First German Protestant Cemetery Society in Cincinnati, Ohio, in 1843 stated, "Really poor persons should be buried in a row of single graves for free. Society members can bury members of their family in their own lot, when they belong to other faiths, but it is not permitted to place a grave marker that is indecent to the protestant society."[16]

Cemetery records may have changed hands if the ownership of a cemetery changed. For example, some Catholic parish cemeteries have come under direction of diocesan offices, which often now house whatever cemetery records were created.

But the records don't always follow cemetery ownership. The Old Baptist Cemetery in Plymouth, Michigan, founded in 1845, was eventually taken over by the city government. According to a local history museum website, many bodies were moved and many tombstones have disappeared. The original burial register created by the church is not with the local government but is at Plymouth Historical Museum.[17]

---

16  Jeffrey Herbert, ed. *Hamilton County, Ohio Burial Records, Volume 13 (German Translations of) First German Protestant Cemetery of Avonsdale & Martini United Church of Christ Records* (Bowie, Md.: Heritage Books, Inc., 2001), xi.

17  "Old Baptist Cemetery," Plymouth Historical Museum (http://www.plymouthhistory.org/archives/old-baptist-cemetery-.html).

# PART 2

# *The Denominations*

*Chapter 6*

✣

# ANGLICAN/EPISCOPAL

## QUICK STATS

### CHURCH ORGANIZED IN THE U.S.:
1639

### DOMINANT REGIONS:
Southern colonies (British)

### DOMINANT ETHNIC ORIGIN:
English

### AFFILIATED FAITHS:
Protestant Episcopal, Methodist Episcopal

## BACKGROUND

The British government established the Church of England (Anglicanism) successfully in the colonies of Virginia, Maryland, the Carolinas, and Georgia. By 1701 membership was largely concentrated in Virginia and Maryland, though there were a number of successful parishes in the Carolinas too. Everyone was taxed to support the church, and many (Anglican by belief or not) were included in local records.

Anglicanism never prospered in New England or even in other mid-Atlantic colonies. Competing denominations got there first and held their ground. Eventually, however, there were Anglican parishes in all the British colonies.

When the Revolutionary War brought about the end of British rule in the American colonies, it also brought major changes to the British state church. Many loyal to British rule had fled for friendlier shores (such as Canada). But many who wanted to remain part of the Anglican faith stayed. In 1789 Anglican ministers in the United States organized the Protestant Episcopal Church as a province in the Anglican communion (separately governed but acknowledged to be in full communion with the Church of England).

Before the end of slavery in the United States, enslaved African Americans participated to some degree in Anglican/Episcopal church life. The Anglican Church instructed slaveholders at various times to teach enslaved people Christianity and to baptize them. Some slaveholders and missionaries complied; many did not. After the Civil War, African Americans in the South largely left white-dominated churches (such as Episcopalian churches) in favor of primarily black churches.[1]

In 1874 the Reformed Episcopal Church broke off from the Protestant Episcopal Church, but there were no other major schisms until the 20th century. (Find a denominational family tree at http://www.thearda.com/denoms/families/trees/familytree_anglican.asp and a dictionary of Anglican terminology at http://www.redeemeroburg.com/termonology/.) Today the Episcopal Church (http://www.episcopalchurch.org/), as it is now known, claims over 2 million members.

Episcopal parishes (congregations) are presided over by priests known as rectors, whose title is "Reverend." Several parishes make up a geographically bounded diocese, which is presided over by a bishop ("Right Reverend"). There is no Episcopalian tradition of strictly national or ethnic parishes as in American Catholicism, but many congregations have served geographical communities of English, Canadian, or Irish heritage.

Parishes weren't well staffed in the early colonial years, or in remote or lightly Anglicanized areas. Traveling priests may have been assigned to serve several parishes. Eventually, parishes got their own rectors-in-residence; these rectors were eventually assisted in their duties by wardens and vestrymen, who were members of the laity, not ordained clergy.

## ABOUT CONGREGATIONAL RECORDS

See Chapter 4 for an example of instructions given to Episcopal priests for creating records.

***Births, deaths, and burials.*** Birth records generally listed the child's name, parents' names, and the date. Death data could include date and place of death (even if not local), cause of death, date and place of interment, and the age of the deceased. A burial record may mention next-of-kin. Unfortunately, many of these registers didn't survive. Look for them either with parish records or in a separate volume.

***Baptisms and confirmations.*** Churches in the Anglican tradition practice infant baptism, but older children in one family were sometimes all baptized at the same time. Adults could be baptized too. So don't assume a baptismal date is for a newborn. Confirmation generally occurred during the young teen years, but adults could be confirmed too.

Baptisms and confirmations may appear in dedicated lists or in the vestry minutes, which may be in separate volumes. Baptisms may include the names of the infant, parents, and sponsors/godparents (who were often the parents themselves or grandparents), as well as the date and the child's age. Confirmations may just name the candidate, date, and performing minister.

***Marriages.*** Colonial parishes attempted to record all marriages, not just those of professed Anglicans, but that didn't happen in practice. In colonial times, it was generally legal to marry by banns or by license. Couples requested to have the banns read for up to three consecutive weeks at church, the courthouse, or any public gathering place. Banns readings may or may not have been recorded in writing. One instance reads as follows: "Please to Published the Banns of Mattrimony between Robert Howlet and Elizebeth Boone, Both of the Parish of St. John's. I beg the favor to let them be asked once to morrow and twice next Sunday."[2]

The information in most Anglican or Episcopal marriage records is scant: just the couple's names, the date, and sometimes the officiant (which may have been taken for granted in a one-minister

1  Albert J. Raboteau, *Slave Religion: The "Invisible Institution" in the Antebellum South* (New York: Oxford University Press, 1978), ch. 4.

2  Henry C. Peden, comp., *St. John's and St. George's Parish Registers, 1696–1851* (Westminster, Md.: Willow Bend, 2006), undated entry from the 1770s, 133.

parish). Sometimes marriages were performed at a private home or the parish rectory; you may find the location noted.

*Membership.* Lists of communicants included all who were eligible to receive communion (confirmed members). Pre-printed, late-19th-century register books also had a separate listing for parishioners, presumably those who attended the church but were not communicants. These lists may include the names of those admitted (or the name of the head of household and the number from that household) and notes, such as removals to another congregation.

Church discipline or excommunication was rare, for there was wide tolerance of difference in beliefs and behavior (and it was a state church to which everyone was supposed to belong). For instance, one complaint of "unlawful cohabitation" in vestry notes mentioned no punishment.

*Parish taxes (tithes).* Parish vestrymen collected this mandatory tax, which supported the minister, upkeep of churches, and—until after disestablishment (1790 in Virginia)—care of the poor. These were onerous taxes, higher than county taxes, and were widely resented. Lists of these taxes were known as tithable lists. Some of these records appear in vestry books.

*Care for the poor and disabled.* During colonial times, church wardens paid local residents (maybe your ancestors) to care for the poor (maybe your ancestors). For example, the vestry minutes of Truro Parish in Virginia say that William Hall, Junior, was paid 300 pounds of tobacco to maintain a poor man in 1738, and another 200 pounds to care for and eventually bury a poor child.

Church officials also oversaw the forced indentures or apprenticeships of indigent, orphaned (fatherless), or illegitimate children. They collected child support for illegitimate children, sometimes generated by fines against the offending parent(s). These records might be in vestry minutes and/or county court records. For example, a court record might show that a fine was levied on a woman who had a "baseborn" child, with the fine payable to the church wardens. After the Anglican Church was disestablished, this duty transferred to local government officials.

*Land processioning.* Every four years in colonial Virginia, county courts ordered church officials to make sure adjoining landowners walked their shared property boundaries together in the company of witnesses. They resolved border disputes and replaced failing boundary markers like the ones you may have seen in old deeds: "an old elm by the stream." Processioning began in the mid-1660s but had best compliance in the 1700s. The practice continued for a time after the Revolutionary War.

Processioning reports in vestry books or separate volumes may be absent or sparse. Sometimes they simply noted a "quiet processioning" (no disagreements) or that nobody showed up, or that it was done. But sometimes there are more details, especially if there were conflicts.

*Memorials.* Post-mortem biographical tributes weren't a regular part of vestry minutes. But some were written to honor the death of a church official or prominent member, as the below example shows:

> On Thursday the 27th of February died at his House in Baltimore County, after two Days Illness, supposed of the Gout, in his Head and Stomach, Doctor Josias Middlemore in the 73d year of his [age], who came from England in the year 1720. . . . He was . . . a Man of Action and Industry, he acquired himself a pretty good Estate by fair and Lawfull means. . . . He bore with great Patience . . . about 3 years ago the Death of his son and only Child [Francis, mentioned later in the passage by name] in his 19th year. . . . His patience was met with another trial in the Loss of a Considerable Part of his Fortune by the Bankrupcy of a late Merchant in London. . . . His funeral Rites were solemnized on the 20th Instant and a Sermon preached from these words 2 Chron 3 and all Judah and Jerusalem mourned for Josiah.[3]

---

3  Henry C. Peden, comp., *St. John's and St. George's Parish Registers, 1696–1851* (Westminster, Md.: Willow Bend, 1987), 130–31.

*Pew rents.* Church pews were available for rent in many Anglican and, later, Episcopalian churches. Parishioners might pay an annual fee or a lifetime lease, depending on the policy of the church. Some vestry books contain numbered lists of pews rented with names assigned them, the amount due (or past due), and occasionally a map of the pew layout. In some places, this custom was carried on into the early 20th century.

## HOW TO ACCESS MEMBERSHIP RECORDS

The first task is to determine the ancestor's parish. Anglican and early Episcopal churches had geographic boundaries. Published regional or state guides are especially helpful for identifying parish names and boundaries. Examples include the Library of Virginia's *A Hornbook of Virginia History* and *The Anglican Parishes of Loudoun County, Virginia,* by Margaret Lail Hopkins and Nancy Hopkins Phillips. Remember that guides may also exist in article format, such as "South Carolina Episcopal Church Records," by Leland Margaretta and Isabella G. Childs in *South Carolina Historical Magazine* 84 (October 1983): 250–63.

Today, old records are still supposed to remain with the congregations. Anglican records stayed with their churches when they became Episcopalian. Browse parishes at http://www.episcopal church.org/find-a-church/. Enter the current ZIP code for the neighborhood where your ancestor would have attended, or browse by province (a multi-state region) or diocese name (which may be a state or major city). You can also search this database by parish name, but parishes are not necessarily named geographically. Contact parish offices to ask about old records (see Chapter 3 for tips).

Records of defunct churches are generally sent to diocesan archives. A diocese is a district with several parishes in it, presided over by a bishop. Find dioceses and contact information at the website cited in the previous paragraph. Diocesan archives may be able to help you locate existing records.

Many Anglican/Episcopalian records didn't survive, and many surviving records have been transcribed and published. State authorities say that *all* extant records from Virginia and North Carolina have been published. Remember to look for both book and article formats.

Anglican records may also be at state archives, particularly in states where Anglicanism was the state church. For example, the Maryland State Archives has copies of nearly all old parish records for the Washington and Easton dioceses (search at http://speccol.mdarchives.state.md.us/pages/churches/).

The Archives of the Episcopal Church doesn't house parish records, but its website does advise researchers on how to contact parish offices and make inquiries (http://www.episcopalarchives.org/genealogy.html). These tips are consistent with those offered earlier in this book, with one interesting exception: "If possible . . . offer to visit the parish to perform the research yourself."

You may get lucky and discover that the Anglican or Episcopal records you're seeking have been put online. It's worth running searches in your favorite web browser with the keywords "Episcopal," "Anglican," "records," "genealogy," and the state, diocese, and parish to which your ancestor belonged. For example, FamilySearch has collections of Episcopal records for Buffalo, New York, and for a church in Galion (Crawford County), Ohio. Ancestry has collections for the Episcopal Dioceses of Spokane, Washington; New York; and New Jersey.

## OTHER RECORDS OF INTEREST

*Parish miscellany.* Anglican parishes also kept records on their own property and expenses; tobacco inspections; and ferry operations and parochial schools (which weren't common and didn't include individual student records). These records may include vestrymen, wardens, major church benefactors, those hired by the church to do work, those involved in tobacco production or ferries, or even an Anglican minister who may have supplemented his income by opening a parish school.

***Diocesan journals.*** These journals record church doings on a diocesan level. For example, the annual *Diocese of Northern Indiana Journal of the Annual Council* lists ministers in each parish, some parish annual history summaries, financial support, membership statistics, delegates to conferences, and more. Ask at the diocesan office about the availability and name of diocesan journals for your family's time period. These can prove helpful if you are trying to understand the life of a parish. They may also help locate the parish to which a minister belonged, if you know the name of the minister who married your ancestor (from county marriage records). The diocesan office may be willing to look up his parish.

***Information on ministers and missionaries.*** The Archives of the Episcopal Church may be able to help you learn more about ancestors who were ministers or missionaries. "Though the Archives does not collect biographical data on all of the Church's clergy, directories kept by the Archives can frequently provide a rough outline of ministerial service and sometimes provide vital information," states its genealogy webpage, referenced on page 60. "Information we may be able to provide includes: date and location of birth, parents' names, education, ordination dates, spouse's name and number of children, and the dates and locations of all the places the priest served. Please note that there will be much less personal information for priests who lived prior to 1920." Some documentation is also available on foreign missionaries.

The *Episcopal Church Annual*, which began in 1830 and continues today, published obituaries the year after a minister died. So did *The Clerical Directory of the Protestant Episcopal Church in the United States of America*, an annual that ran from 1898 to 1968. *A List of Emigrant Ministers to America, 1690–1811,* by Gerald Fothergill, extracts names of Church of England ministers from documents in the British Public Record Office (The National Archives).

Colonial-era missionaries for the Church of England served under the Society for the Propagation of the Gospel (SPG). These records are at the Bodleian Library's Weston Library building (moved there from their previous location at Rhodes House) in Oxford, England (https://www.bodleian.ox.ac.uk/weston).

Newspapers were not as popular among Anglicans and Episcopalians as they were among some other U.S. denominations. That said, some dioceses had their own papers. A handful appear in Chronicling America's U.S. Newspaper Directory (https://chroniclingamerica.loc.gov/), including *Churchman* (N.Y., 1831–1861) and *Episcopal Register* (Pa., 1870–1884). Consult these largely for ministers' memorials rather than newsy tidbits or obituaries of everyday members.

## FURTHER READING

Bellamy, V. Nelle. "Church Records of the United States, Part B, Part IV, Protestant Episcopal." 7 pp. World Conference on Records: Written, Oral and Traditional History in the USA and Canada as Applied to Research; Genealogical Society of The Church of Jesus Christ of Latter-day Saints. This collection of brief printed talks from 1969 is held at the Genealogy Center, Allen County Public Library, Fort Wayne, Ind.

Holmes, David L. *A Brief History of the Episcopal Church.* Valley Forge, Pa.: Trinity Press International, 1993.

*Lloyd's Clerical Directory for 1898 . . . Protestant Episcopal Church in the United States of America.* Hamilton, Ohio: News and Telegraph Publishing Company, 1898.

Pritchard, Robert W. *A History of the Episcopal Church,* 3rd ed. New York: Morehouse Publishing, 2014.

# Chapter 7

✠

## BAPTIST

### QUICK STATS

**FIRST ARRIVED IN THE U.S.:**
1630s

**DOMINANT REGIONS:**
South; Rhode Island and mid-Atlantic during the colonial era

**DOMINANT ETHNIC GROUPS:**
English, Scots-Irish, African-American

**AFFILIATED FAITHS:**
Any church with "Baptist" in its name

## BACKGROUND

In 1638 Roger Williams established the first Baptist church in the British colonies in what is now Rhode Island. By 1707 the Philadelphia Baptist Association formed from congregations in New Jersey and Pennsylvania. By the end of the century, the Baptist Church claimed 60,000 members in 750 churches across 35 Baptist associations.

Baptist churches continued to grow throughout the late colonial era and well into the 1800s. The Baptists opposed state influence over religion, championed personal choice, and built strong, locally run congregations, all of which resonated well with the democratic ideals of the emerging nation. Descendants of Scots-Irish settlers, who arrived as Presbyterians and populated Appalachia, often became Baptist or Methodist.

By the mid-1800s, the Baptists and Methodists dominated U.S. denominations, especially across the South from Florida to Texas. This trend continued into the 1900s. The 1926 U.S. census of religious bodies counted 23,374 Southern Baptist congregations; 22,081 "Negro Baptist" congregations; and 7,611 Northern Baptist congregations, which together comprised almost 23 percent of total U.S. congregations.[1]

---

1 Department of Commerce and Labor, Bureau of the Census, *Census of Religious Bodies, 1926, Part I: Summary and Detailed Tables* (Washington, D.C.: Government Printing Office, 1930), 13–14 (http://www2.census.gov/prod2/decennial/documents/13949806v1ch1.pdf).

There has been some splintering of Baptist associations (regional organizations) and conventions (even larger umbrella organizations) over time. The Philadelphia Baptist Association divided for a time into "Old Lights" and "New Lights" in the mid-1700s but reunited as the Baptist Missionary Convention in 1814. That group split into the Northern Baptist Convention and the Southern Baptist Convention over slavery in the mid-1840s. Today, the Southern Baptist Convention claims over 16 million members, concentrated in the South. The Northern Baptist Convention eventually became today's American Baptist Churches USA, with 1.3 million members.

From the ranks of Baptists emerged several historically African-American churches. Those with the largest membership today include the National Baptist Convention of America, the National Missionary Baptist Convention of America, and the National Baptist Convention, USA. See a Baptist denominational tree at http://www.thearda.com/Denoms/Families/trees/familytree_baptist.asp.

## ABOUT CONGREGATIONAL RECORDS

Baptist records tend to be relatively few in number and sparse in genealogical content. Those that were created may not have been preserved, or may be archived in scattered locations. Baptist membership records generally include less genealogical information than those of other major U.S. faiths.

That said, for some times, places, and people (especially poor Southerners and Appalachians), few records of *any* kind may exist. So it may be worth looking for *all* possible records, including Baptist meeting records, newspapers, and histories.

***Business meeting proceedings.*** The core Baptist congregational records are proceedings of the business meetings, akin to congregational minutes in other faiths. Genealogical details are more likely to be buried in narrative proceedings than conveniently (for us) arranged in alphabetical lists, though some lists do exist. But taken as a whole, the meeting notes may spell out just the details you need to reconstruct a family unit or part of an ancestor's life story.

***Vital events.*** The Southern Baptist Historical Library and Archives (SBHLA) website states that births, marriages, and deaths are not included in its denominational records (see more at http://www.sbhla.org/familyhistory.htm). You may find exceptions to that rule. You might get lucky and find a list of deaths, such as the one in the records of the Regular Baptist Church in Chardon, Ohio.[2] The list is faded and difficult to read, but there are columns for the person's name; month, day, and year of death; and—crammed into the far right margin—age at death.

Marriages were not generally recorded, as they are not considered a religious vow. According to one expert on Baptist records, "Evidences of marriage can sometimes be deduced, however, from the dismissal of members to a sister church, in which the wife's maiden name may be mentioned in that proceeding, or her name on the roll may be corrected by lining out in the membership records."[3]

***Membership data.*** Mentions of members may appear within proceedings in narrative or list format. Often, all you will find are names and dates, perhaps alongside other family members. Look for husbands and wives listed together in the business meetings proceedings, though it's possible you may just read about "Thomas Humphrey and wife."

Admissions and dismissions (by departure or death) may be indicated by a short note next to a member's name on a list, sometimes without dates or places. Hints about migrations may also

2   Records of the Regular Baptist Church, Chardon, Ohio, 1862–1903; MSS 542, Western Reserve Historical Society, Cleveland.
3   F. Wilbur Helmbold, "Baptist Records," Church Records of the United States, Part A, Part IV, page 3, in World Conference on Records and Genealogical Seminar. Salt Lake City, Utah, 5–8 August, 1969. This collection of brief printed talks is held at the Genealogy Center, Allen County Public Library, Fort Wayne, Ind.

appear in the conference proceedings. You may see when someone was admitted or when he left. If the admission was via letter (meaning they were already Baptists coming from another congregation), then you're likely looking at a recent move-in and the letter might say from what town or congregation. Admission by profession of a personal conversion experience would more likely be for people who had been local residents for a time. If someone was dismissed to another congregation, the name of his new town or church may be mentioned.

*Baptisms.* Baptists do not practice infant baptism. Members could be baptized as early as the young teen years. When baptisms were recorded, they did not generally list ages or names of parents. Since babies weren't baptized, you can't make any assumptions about someone's age from baptismal records, except that the person was not a young child. Baptismal records are rare but occasionally may be found among congregational records.

*Conduct and discipline.* The efforts of preachers and dedicated laypeople are detailed in congregational proceedings. You may see lists of auxiliary members, volunteers, and subscribers to specific causes. You may see memorial tributes to prominent ministers or influential members after their deaths.

Bad behavior was often noted too. Members could be disciplined for a variety of reasons, including fighting, conducting business on Sunday, neglecting church attendance or duties, or having a child out of wedlock. The most extreme form of discipline was exclusion. However, it's not uncommon to read about a repentant soul who was later restored to the fold.

## HOW TO FIND AND ORDER MEMBERSHIP RECORDS

It's possible to start by contacting existing Baptist congregations where your ancestor lived. However, Baptist churches are so numerous (and sometimes so small and off-the-grid) that this may not be the best approach. Instead, start with strategies from Chapter 2 to identify local congregation(s) that existed there during your ancestor's time. Then ask local historical and genealogical societies whether such records still exist and, if so, where.

Another approach to locating original Baptist records is to contact the archives of state Baptist conventions, state archives, and university archival collections. Find helpful directories to these at the websites of Baylor University (https://www.baylor.edu/baptiststudies/index.php?id=94593) and the SBHLA (http://www.sbhla.org/links.htm).

Some libraries have online finding aids for church records in their holdings. The SBHLA, the denominational archive for the largest U.S. Baptist organization, holds microfilmed records for member churches, listed by state, at http://www.sbhla.org/churchrecords.asp. The American Baptist Historical Society has an online inventory of its church records too; find a link at http://abhsarchives.org/for-researchers/. Search the websites of other Baptist archives for similar information.

Knowing an ancestor's ethnicity may make it easier to identify existing records, whether you're searching online or speaking to a librarian. The American Baptist Historical Society houses denominational minutes for Danish, Norwegian, Swedish, German, Italian, and Slovakian immigrant congregations. It offers an online research guide for researching African-American church associations at the same link mentioned in the previous paragraph.

The SBHLA has a wealth of black Baptist church records and other materials on microfilm. Conducting a web search for "Baptist," the state, and the ethnicity can bring up materials like the online finding aid at the Library of Virginia (https://www.lva.virginia.gov/public/guides/African_American_Churches.pdf) for African-American church manuscript records, histories, association and convention materials, and more.

Finally, try to identify which Baptist association your ancestor may have belonged to, using historical resources such as the *Encyclopedia of Southern Baptists* (digitized at http://digitalcollections. baylor.edu/cdm/landingpage/collection/ml-encsb) or conversations with state archivists. Then look for historical material relating to that association and/or its ministers (if you can determine their names). Helpful resources may include the following:

- Published inventories, such as *Inventory of the Church Records of North Carolina: Yancey Baptist Association,* which was published as part of the WPA Historical Records Survey and can be read on Internet Archive (https://www.archive.org).

- Edwin C. Starr's *A Baptist Bibliography (1952),* searchable at http://www.baptistheritage. com/starr-baptist-bibliography. There's an ongoing bibliographical project covering more recent works on "all things Baptist" at https://www.baylor.edu/baptiststudies/index. php?id=97479.

- WorldCat, ArchiveGrid, and PERSI (see Chapter 3).

## OTHER RECORDS OF INTEREST

Baptist congregations may have kept other records, depending on the time period, their zeal, and their organizing skills. You may find Sunday School books, financial records, and women's auxiliary records. Other useful records are listed below.

***Baptist newspapers.*** These have been published on the state level in various times and places. Some Baptist sects published obituaries for everyday members, not just prominent ones. State Baptist archives generally have runs of their own newspapers. Some archives or library collections may have online inventories of newspapers and other publications.

One quick way to search for specific newspaper titles is to use the U.S. Newspaper Directory at Chronicling America (http://chroniclingamerica.loc.gov/search/titles/). Search by state; adding the keyword "Baptist" may help. Individual papers' entries should include a list of libraries that hold them.

Some Baptist newspapers have been microfilmed. You may be able to borrow them via interlibrary loan from university collections. Few have been digitized; find them at http://www.baptist heritage.com/digital-library/.

***Ministers' personal records.*** Ministers' correspondence, logs, or diaries may mention ancestors or daily doings of their community. But many pastors didn't keep such records and many more have been lost over time. Surviving original manuscript records may be buried in an archive under the pastor's name. Use your best sleuthing skills to search online manuscript catalogs. An online bibliography of ministerial manuscripts at the Colgate Library (http://abhsarchives.org/ wp-content/uploads/2014/04/ColgateManuscripts.pdf) offers a sense of the kinds of papers that may exist relating to a Baptist minister.

Other records may be helpful when researching pastors and influential church members:

- *Association proceedings or minutes.* The minutes of regional meetings mention pastors and delegates from each congregation. They may also include brief histories of individual congregations and biographies of notable ministers. Associations used to be geographically larger than they are today, so trace the history of association membership in resources like the *Encyclopedia of Southern Baptists.*

- *State convention records.* Particularly within the Southern Baptist Convention, congregations also belong to larger regional groups known as state conventions. Again, the minutes of their meetings mention ordained ministers. They can also be helpful when tracing association memberships over time.

- *Major convention records.* Many Baptist congregations also are connected to an even larger Baptist convention, such as the Southern Baptist Convention or American Baptist Convention. The conventions' proceedings can help you locate ministers who moved. Southern Baptist Convention Annuals (1845–2013) are digitized at http://www.sbhla. org/digital_resources.asp.

- *Scholarly papers.* There may be a book, article, or dissertation on a pastor or congregation. Search for these in WorldCat and PERSI, with the keywords "Baptist" or the name of the congregation, minister, town, and state, as needed.

***Missionary records.*** Baptist missionaries served both at home and abroad in the 1800s and 1900s. "If your ancestor served as a Southern Baptist foreign or home missionary, there is a good chance that the collection contains some biographical information files and perhaps some correspondence," states the SBHLA website. The SBHLA also houses the official records of the Home Mission Board and Foreign Mission Board, along with other denominational agencies. Read more and learn how to make a family history research request at http://www.sbhla.org/familyhistory. htm.

***Cemetery records.*** Many Baptist churches have had cemeteries at some point in their history. When asking about Baptist records, always ask specifically about any cemetery records. As stated in an earlier chapter, these may have been transferred to a local repository or given to a cemetery's new owners. The SBHLA suggests that congregations have their cemetery records microfilmed. That doesn't always happen, but it's worth watching for.

## FURTHER READING

"Baptist Churches," pp. 42–67 in Frank S. Mead and Samuel S. Hill, *Handbook of Denominations in the United States,* 11th ed. Nashville: Abingdon Press, 2001.

Helmbold, F. Wilbur. "Baptist records for genealogy and history," *National Genealogical Society Quarterly,* 61 (Sept 1973):168–78.

Helmbold, F. Wilbur. "Family History in the Bible Belt: Southern U.S. Church Records," in *World Conference on Records: Preserving Our Heritage,* vol. 3, part 1 (Salt Lake City?: The Church of Jesus Christ of Latter-day Saints, 1980).

Rudolph, L. C. "Baptists," pp. 37–60 in *Hoosier Faiths: A History of Indiana Churches & Religious Groups.* Bloomington: Indiana University Press, 1995. This and comparable books for other states and regions provide context for the records, focusing on what our ancestors believed and what they argued about.

## Chapter 8

# CONGREGATIONAL

### QUICK STATS

#### FIRST ARRIVED IN THE U.S.:
1620

#### DOMINANT REGIONS:
New England

#### DOMINANT ETHNIC ORIGIN:
English

#### AFFILIATED FAITHS:
Presbyterian, Unitarian, Universalist, Disciples of Christ, Evangelical
and Reformed, United Church of Christ

## BACKGROUND

Congregationalism arose from the doctrines and culture of the English Puritans, who opposed the practices and organization of the Church of England (Anglican Church). As the name implies, Congregationalists believed that a local congregation should govern itself, not submit to a hierarchy of superior governing bodies. Congregational members entered into a mutual covenant and shared decision-making authority with their local minister. Throughout the colonial era, most churches required prospective members to relate personal conversion experiences to be admitted. Members could be censured or even expelled for inappropriate behaviors.

Congregational churches were state-supported in much of colonial New England. Many churches continued to be supported by taxpayers even after the Revolutionary War (in Connecticut until 1818 and Massachusetts until 1833).

Congregationalism didn't flourish on the frontier, with the exception of some areas that were heavily populated by New Englanders, such as the Connecticut Western Reserve (northeast Ohio). However, Presbyterianism did flourish, and for several decades in the early 1800s, congregations of these two faiths united in many places. For this reason, sometimes you can find Congregationalist ancestors in the registers of frontier Presbyterian churches and vice versa. If the churches eventually divided again, you may find old records archived with either congregation.

Some Congregational churches split off to create the American Unitarian Association in 1825. That organization later joined with the Universalist Church in America to become the Unitarian Universalist Association in 1961.

A number of charitable organizations formed within the Congregational Church in the 1800s, especially ones for women. These ranged from local sewing circles to groups with wider influence: the American Board of Commissioners for Foreign Missions (1810); American Home Missionary Society (1826); American Education Society (originally the American Society for the Education of Pious Youth) (1815); American Missionary Association (1846); and others.

In the 1930s, Congregationalist churches merged with some from the Disciples of Christ to become the Congregational Christian Churches. In the 1950s, the main body of Congregational Christian Churches merged with the Evangelical and Reformed Church to become the United Church of Christ. Those who rejected that merger created the National Association of Congregational Christian Churches. Find a denominational tree of Congregationalism online at http://www.thearda.com/denoms/families/trees/familytree_unitedcoc.asp.

## ABOUT CONGREGATIONAL RECORDS

Early Congregational church records were handwritten; their content and completeness varies according to the attention paid by the ministers who usually kept them. The first volume of records often contained information about the formation of the church, charter members' names, and minutes of its activities. Running lists of members and baptisms may appear at the back of these books. You may also find lists of members recorded periodically and interspersed with the chronological notes.

By the late 1800s, some churches began using preprinted register books (often *The American Church Register*) with dedicated pages and columns for lists of communicants, baptisms, marriages, deaths, attendance, contributions, and more. These were often not completely filled out, but they did usually have some information.

*Vital events and relationships.* Vital events and relationships are, unfortunately, not often detailed in Congregational records. Births are often not recorded at all. You may find lists of marriages with the names and residences of the bride and groom, the date of the wedding, and the name of the person who performed it. Parents' and spouses' names are sometimes found in baptismal records and in individual membership records (see below).

The most likely place to find members' deaths is in the membership list or register (see below). These may appear at the end of the members' entries where you'd otherwise find information about their dismissal (how they left the church). You may find an age and/or date of death.

Occasionally you may find brief mention in minutes about the deaths of prominent members, like this one: "May 1st, 1879, Capt. Jessee Smith died . . . Having been an active member of this church for more than fifty years."[1]

*Membership data.* Membership lists are usually the best place to find genealogical data in Congregational church records. For each person, you might find the following:

- A name and sometimes a woman's former or maiden name
- Admission information: when he or she joined the church and how admitted (by letter or confession of faith), and a prior congregational affiliation

---

1   Records of the West Church Haverhill vol. 6, 1870–1880, p. 99 original, p. 205 digital; *Congregational Library and Archives: History Matters* > Haverhill, Mass. West Parish Congregational Church (http://www.congregationallibrary.org/nehh/series1/Haverhill MAWest5067) > Church Records, 1870–1880.

- Dismission information to another congregation, which may include a date, mention of a letter given, and the location or name of the new congregation

- A comments column with an address or a note; for example, "wife of Abraham Bently" or "married to N.H Brooks, June 14, 1893"

Finally, members could be disciplined by the church for their behavior. See the section below describing minute books for records relating to church discipline and expulsion.

*Baptisms.* Ministers often recorded lists of baptisms for both adults and children. Baptism was not required but was encouraged. Baptisms of adults may only mention names and dates, and possibly the name of a woman's husband. Children's baptisms usually name the parents, at least the father. Sometimes several children in the same family were baptized at the same time and listed together, a boon for reconstructing family groups. A mother presenting a child for baptism may be identified as a widow.

Occasionally, baptismal lists offer more detailed tidbits about an ancestral family, like this passage dated October 24, 1725: "Nathan Gurney and his wife owned by Covenant [or joined the church by entering into a covenant] and made an acknowledgement of the sin of fornication and had their daughter Martha baptized."[2]

See examples of Congregationalist records in Chapter 1.

## HOW TO ACCESS MEMBERSHIP RECORDS

Use the methods outlined in Chapter 2 to identify your ancestor's congregation. Then go to the Congregational Library's Reference Desk webpage (http://www.congregationallibrary.org/researchers/ref-desk) for links to indexes and inventories to extant original church records. Among the invaluable resources you'll find there are *An Inventory of the Records of the Particular (Congregational) Churches in Massachusetts, Gathered 1620–1805*, by Harold Field Worthley, as well as a series of volumes by Richard H. Taylor that detail historical changes in Congregational churches (mergers, closings, and name changes) for the South, West, mid-Atlantic, Great Lakes, and Plains regions. These volumes can help you determine whether records still exist and how to pursue them.

Here are some additional strategies for finding Congregational church records:

- The Congregational Library (http://www.congregationallibrary.org/) has thousands of original and microfilmed records. The library has an online catalog; click Catalog from the home page. It also has a growing digital archive of manuscript church records on its website (under Digital Collections). Visit http://www.congregationallibrary.org/nehh/series1 for a list of specific church record collections for Massachusetts, some of which have been transcribed.

- Government archives hold some original records. An example is the Connecticut State Library (https://ctstatelibrary.org/). Remember, Congregationalism used to be supported by the government. The New Hampshire Historical Society (https://www.nhhistory.org) and Maine Historical Society (https://www.mainehistory.org/) also hold Congregational records.

- Use online manuscript finding aids such as ArchiveGrid (https://researchworks.oclc.org/archivegrid/) to track down original records, especially in New England repositories.

---

2  Abington Church Book 1724 to 1729, unpaginated, digital p. 36; *Congregational Library and Archives: History Matters* > Abington, Mass., First Congregational Church > Church Records, 1714–1749 (http://www.congregationallibrary.org/nehh/series1/Abington MAFirst).

- A large number of Congregational records have been published or microfilmed. The FamilySearch Catalog (https://www.famlysearch.org/search/catalog/search) and WorldCat (http://www.worldcat.org/) can help locate these. Digitized versions of some Congregational church records are now on Internet Archive, HathiTrust, and other digital archives; find these by searching on the name of the church and its location.

The Congregational Library has collected (or at least has access to) all known colonial-era conversion narratives. These were the personal experiences given by new church members and sometimes transcribed by the minister and presented to the congregation for examination and approval. Though rare, it's worth browsing the library's church record collections to learn whether an ancestor penned one, or even just to get a flavor for their content.

Many historical Congregational churches are now affiliated with other denominations, most notably the following:

- *The United Church of Christ (UCC).* The UCC does archive materials relating to its member churches, but not historical records that pre-date their affiliation with UCC. Contacting UCC archives is generally not productive when looking for old Congregational records.

- *Churches from the Unitarian Universalist tradition.* Contact local churches to see whether they have records from the right time period, or consult the Andover-Harvard Theological Library webpage (http://library.hds.harvard.edu/collections/special-collections/manuscripts-archives).

## OTHER RECORDS OF INTEREST

If you locate membership records for an ancestral church, ask the custodians of these records whether any of the following may be available.

*Minute books.* These books often include detailed accounts of church and community affairs, and can teach a lot about daily life during the time period. Page through any surviving minute books, watching for mention of your ancestor participating in church activities or even being disciplined. For example, in the deacon's minutes of the Abington Church in Massachusetts, a note dated August 31, 1736, stated that "Elizabeth Turrell Widow was laid under Suspension & Admonition for the sin of fornication."[3]

*Financial records.* Pew rentals, donation lists, and subscription lists are among the types of financial records that may name your Congregational ancestor. Entries may be dated, confirming your ancestor's residence there at that time. They may also mention details of your ancestor's life, such as the amount of a donation or a note that your ancestor didn't follow through on a contribution promise.

*Additional local administrative records and histories.* The original record book created when a congregation was organized often included its creed or core beliefs; a written statement of the covenant into which new members entered; and rules of conduct that members were expected to follow. Local histories of the church may also have been written.

*Ministerial/conference records.* If your ancestor was a minister or other church officer, it may be worth looking for him in minutes of general, annual, and special meetings of the regional Congregational conference. One particularly helpful resource is *The Congregational Yearbook*, published annually since 1854. It includes lists of ministers, obituaries of ministers who recently died, and statistics on local congregations. The Congregational Library has links to all Congregational

---

3 Abington Church Book 1724 to 1729, unpaginated, digital p. 11; *Congregational Library and Archives: History Matters* > Abington, Mass., First Congregational Church > Church Records, 1714–1749 (http://www.congregationallibrary.org/nehh/series1/Abington MAFirst).

yearbooks at http://www.congregationallibrary.org/periodicals/yearbooks. You may find print versions at major research libraries. An online index to ministers' and missionaries' obituaries is searchable for free at http://www.congregationallibrary.org/for-researchers/search-obituaries.

## FURTHER READING

Matthews, Barbara Jean. *The Demanding Genealogist* > Connecticut Columns > "Congregational Church Records in Connecticut," 22 May 2000 (downloadable version linked to at https://www.demandinggenealogist.com/publications.html).

Pope, Robert G. *The Half-Way Covenant: Church Membership in Puritan New England.* Princeton, N.J.: Princeton University Press, 1969.

Von Rohr, John. *The Shaping of American Congregationalism, 1620–1957.* Cleveland: Pilgrim's Press, 1992.

Walker, Williston, *Creeds and Platforms of Congregationalism.* New York: Pilgrim's Press, 1991.

*Chapter 9*

# DUTCH REFORMED/REFORMED CHURCH IN AMERICA

## QUICK STATS

### FIRST ARRIVED IN THE U.S.:
1628

### DOMINANT REGIONS:
New Amsterdam/New York, New Jersey, Pennsylvania, Midwest

### DOMINANT ETHNIC ORIGIN:
Dutch

### AFFILIATED FAITHS:
Reformed Church in America (RCA), Christian Reformed Church,
German Reformed, Lutheran, Presbyterian

## BACKGROUND

The first permanent Dutch settlers in North America arrived in 1624. They put down roots in what is now Albany, New York, and along the Delaware River, which now separates New Jersey from Pennsylvania. Within four years, the first Dutch Reformed congregation was organized in what is now New York City.

Initially, Dutch Reformed congregations were state-sponsored churches under the Dutch colonial government. When the English government took over New Netherland in 1664, the colonial churches continued their affiliation with the mother church in Holland—and continued to grow and thrive. The American Revolution saw divided loyalties among Dutch Reformed church members. Many Loyalists fled north via central New York and started churches along the St. Lawrence River.

During the 1600s and 1700s, Dutch Reformed ministers in many places also served German Reformed parishioners who did not yet have German-speaking ministers. (Their theology was the same, and their languages mutually intelligible.)

In 1819 the Reformed Protestant Dutch Church incorporated in the United States. However, Dutch language and culture generally diminished during the 1800s, despite another wave of Dutch immigrants in 1847 who settled in Iowa and Michigan. In 1857 several congregations seceded to form the Christian Reformed Church.

After the Civil War, the Reformed Protestant Dutch Church assumed yet another new name: the Reformed Church in America (as distinct from the German-heritage Reformed Church in the United States). The Reformed Protestant Dutch Church did retain the support of many Dutch immigrants and their descendants, including many in the Midwest and parts of Canada. As New Englanders came to New York, they often joined Reformed and Presbyterian churches.

Congregations from this tradition are governed by a consistory consisting of elders and deacons. The elders are responsible for the spiritual aspects of the congregation and the deacons are responsible for the physical and economic needs of the congregation. The pastor leads and is accountable to the classis (regional governing body). In this tradition, the classis has the authority to organize and disband churches and ordain and install pastors.

## ABOUT CONGREGATIONAL RECORDS

The Dutch Reformed tradition practices infant baptism but will also baptize children and adults who have not received a valid Christian baptism. Sprinkling is the most common, but not the only accepted, mode of baptism. Godparents are often relatives. Adults who join with the church also make a public confession or profession of faith in Christ, which may be mentioned in the consistory records (see below).

*Baptisms.* These commonly include the name of the person baptized, along with his or her parents' names, and the date, place, and officiant at the baptism. For adult baptisms, parents' names may not be mentioned; the date and place of birth may be. Occasionally, you find remarks such as the circumstances of emergency baptisms performed for the sick; dismissals to another church; or a note that only one parent approved the baptism ("on responsibility of the mother only").

*Marriages.* In the Reformed tradition, marriage is not considered a sacrament, but Dutch churches did keep marriage records. Look for the date of marriage and names of the bride and groom. You may also find their ages, birthplaces, places of residence, and occupations. The reading (or dispensation) of banns was required before 1664; after that time, a couple could apply for a license instead of banns. Women often continued to use their maiden names after marriage.

*Records of deaths.* Records of death (and sometimes funerals and/or burials) commonly include the name of the deceased as well as the place and date of death. You may also find the deceased's gender, place of residence, age at death, marital status, location of funeral service, place of burial, and next of kin. Occasionally, the birthplace and birth date of the deceased are noted.

*Membership lists.* These may exist; they may be organized chronologically (for larger bodies, by first letter of surname). Look for the date of admittance, how admitted (by confession or certificate of transfer), and date and type of removal (generally by death or by dismissal/letter of transfer to another church, which may be identified). A column with additional remarks may mention family relationships ("wife of . . ."), age at death, or status in the church (founding member, deacon, etc). See an example of a transfer letter on page 9.

*Consistory minutes.* These document the everyday affairs and governance of individual congregations. They may include information about new members and those who transferred in or out of the congregation. It was the responsibility of church elders to exercise discipline and to admit members to the church. In some cases, *elders' minutes* exist, and these may provide information about membership and baptisms if register books do not exist.

Older church records were kept in the language of the congregation, often Dutch. You may also come across Dutch patronymic or naming customs, which can help identify additional relatives. Furthermore, some Dutch surnames have specific regional origins in the Netherlands. The Family-Search wiki (https://www.familysearch.org/wiki) has articles that may prove invaluable: in the main search box, enter "Dutch research introduction" to find a get-started article and discussion of naming traditions, or "Dutch genealogical word list" for translations of common terminology.

## HOW TO ACCESS MEMBERSHIP RECORDS

Today, congregations of the Dutch Reformed tradition generally maintain their records locally. Use online church locator tools to connect with current congregations of the Reformed Church in America (https://www.rca.org/church-finder) and the Christian Reformed Church (https://www.crcna.org/church-finder).

That said, many older Dutch Reformed records have been gathered by central archives, and some have been published in print and/or online. The subscription website Ancestry (https://www.ancestry.com) has these major collections:

- "U.S., Dutch Christian Reformed Church Membership Records, 1856–1970" (http://search.ancestry.com/search/db.aspx?dbid=60767);
- "U.S., Dutch Christian Reformed Church Vital Records, 1856–1970" (http://search.ancestry.com/search/db.aspx?dbid=60524);
- "U.S., Dutch Reformed Church Records in Selected States, 1639–1989" (http://search.ancestry.com/search/db.aspx?dbid=6961);
- "U.S., Selected States Dutch Reformed Church Membership Records, 1701–1995" (http://search.ancestry.com/search/db.aspx?dbid=60766).

The Archives of the Christian Reformed Church in America (http://www.calvin.edu/hh/crc_archives.htm) strives to collect and image original records, returning them to the church's congregations. Many of these have been included in the first two Ancestry databases mentioned above. Records since about 1950 are restricted.

The website of the Archives of the Reformed Church in America (https://www.rca.org/rca-basics/archives) has a link to "Guide to Local Church Records in the Archives of the Reformed Church in America and Other Repositories" (http://images.rca.org/docs/archives/church records.pdf), compiled by Russell L. Gasero and Erica McLaughin. The authors refer to this as a draft guide since it has not been updated, but it's still of value. Many collections at the Archives of the Reformed Church in America have been digitized and indexed in the third and fourth Ancestry databases mentioned above.

The Holland Society of New York (http://www.hollandsociety.org) maintains a library on the people and history of New Netherland, as well as other Dutch migrations in North America. Among its holdings are over 100 volumes of Dutch Reformed church records of births, marriages, and death for present-day New York, New Jersey, and Pennsylvania. These have been digitized and indexed in the third Ancestry database referenced above.

The Holland Society has also published several volumes of Dutch Reformed records for select New York and New Jersey congregations. The records of the Albany church were originally transcribed and published in several annual volumes of the *Holland Society Year Book*. These were compiled and reprinted as *Records of the Reformed Dutch Church of Albany, New York* (Genealogical Publishing, 1978); a third-party index (1683–1809) was created at https://mathcs.clarku.edu/~djoyce/gen/albany/refchurch.html.

The library of the New England Historic Genealogical Society (https://www.americanancestors.org) has both manuscript and published Dutch Reformed records for various churches in New York, New Jersey, and elsewhere. Searching its online catalog is free; membership is required to access its databases of Dutch Reformed congregational and newspaper records.

The New York Public Library's Archives & Manuscripts Division (http://archives.nypl.org/) has a considerable collection of Dutch Reformed church records for New York. Less focused on church records per se but still worth noting is the New Netherland Research Center at the New York State Library (https://www.newnetherlandinstitute.org/), which has a significant collection of manuscript and published records on colonial Dutch life.

Another resource, this one specific to New York City, is Harry Macy, Jr.'s *Reformed Church Records of New York City (Manhattan and Bronx)*, first published in 1994 and updated to 2017, available at https://www.newyorkfamilyhistory.org/knowledgebase/reformed-church-records-new-york-city-manhattan-bronx. Access requires membership in the New York Genealogical and Biographical Society, but if you have Dutch roots in New York, you will likely benefit from joining in any case. Macy's knowledge of New York City is without peer; there are cross-references and analyses of other boroughs and record sets too.

A must-consult resource for finding records in print is David M. Riker's four-volume set, *Genealogical and Biographical Directory to Persons in New Netherland, from 1613 to 1674*. This resource is especially helpful for trying to tell apart families with a common surname.

In addition, search PERSI (see Chapter 3) for additional Dutch Reformed church record transcriptions that have been published in periodicals such as *The New York Genealogical and Biographical Record* and *Genealogical Magazine of New Jersey*. Published indexes or transcriptions may not include all record types (such as burials) and may not include every piece of information within a specific record. Whenever possible, try to view original records.

## OTHER RECORDS OF INTEREST

*Ministerial records.* Before the American Revolution, ministers were generally ordained and sent by the Dutch Reformed Church leadership in Holland. Deacons were also elected by local church members to carry out local church business, including financial matters, legal issues, and calling new ministers.

A free database of current and past Christian Reformed Church ministers is searchable at (http://www.calvin.edu/library/database/crcmd). It includes full name, birthplace, a photograph, and the minister's current and previous places of service. The same site offers an index to obituaries of ministers' military service-related deaths at http://www.calvin.edu/hh/crc_archives.htm. The publication *Historical Directory of the Christian Reformed Church*, compiled and edited by Richard H. Harms, contains "information about 1,415 ministries, 2,773 ministers, chaplains, evangelists, specialized ministers, mission field workers, synods, classes and more."[1] The many libraries and archives above may have manuscript holdings pertaining to individual ministers.

For information about ministers of the Reformed Church in America, see Russell L. Gasero's *Historical Directory of the Reformed Church in America, 1628–2000*.[2] The volume contains biographies of almost 7,000 ministers who have served in the Reformed Church in America, including information on their careers and the churches they served. In addition, there is a list of nearly 1,700 congregations, their organization dates, and the ministers who served them.

1    Richard H. Harms, comp. and ed., *Historical Directory of the Christian Reformed Church in North America* (Grand Rapids, Mich.: Historical Committee of the Christian Reformed Church in North America, 2004).

2    Russell L. Gasero, *Historical Directory of the Reformed Church in America, 1628–2000* (Grand Rapids, Mich.: Wm. B. Eerdmans, 2000).

The Reformed Church Archives also has an extensive pamphlet collection of sermons, news clippings, and other items about many RCA ministers. Similar materials are also available in the Archives of the Christian Reformed Church.

**Newspapers.** The *Christian Intelligencer* became the *Intelligencer-Leader* and then the *Church Herald*, now online as *RCA Today* (https://www.rca.org/rca-today). Indexes to deaths and marriages in the *Christian Intelligencer* (1830–1871) are available in the members-only area at https://www.americanancestors.org. Hope College maintains an archive of Dutch-language newspapers and those published in the Dutch immigrant community of Holland, Michigan; see https://hope.edu/lib2/joint-archives/collections/newspapers.php for a list of holdings and links to other collections and indexes.

# FURTHER READING

Bailey, Rosalie Fellows. *Dutch Systems in Family Naming: New York–New Jersey.* Special Publication of the National Genealogical Society, No. 12. Washington, D.C.: National Genealogical Society, 1965.

Balmer, Randall. *A Perfect Babel of Confusion: Dutch Religion and English Culture in the Middle Colonies.* New York: Oxford University Press, 2002.

DeJong, Gerald F. *The Dutch Reformed Church in the American Colonies,* Book 5 in *Historical Series of the Reformed Church in America.* Grand Rapids, Mich.: Eerdmans Publishing Co., 1978.

Epperson, Gwen F. "Early Dutch Church Marriages Registers and Other Church Records," in *New Netherland Roots,* 10–19. Baltimore, Md.: Clearfield Co., 2008.

Fabend, Firth. *A Dutch Family in the Middle Colonies: 1660–1800.* New Brunswick, N.J.: Rutgers University Press, 1999.

Fabend, Firth. *New Netherland in a Nutshell.* Albany, N.Y.: New Netherland Institute, 2012.

Fabend, Firth. *Zion on the Hudson. Dutch New York and New Jersey in the Age of Revivals.* New Brunswick, N.J.: Rutgers University Press, 2000.

Hoff, Henry B. "Researching Dutch Families in New York and New Jersey." *de Halve Maen* 82:4 (Winter 2009), 67–70.

Riker, David M. *Genealogical and Biographical Directory to Persons in New Netherland, from 1613 to 1674,* 4 vols. + supplement. Salem, Mass.: Higginson Book Co., 2000.

Stryker-Rodda, Kenn. "New Netherland Naming Systems and Customs." *The New York Genealogical and Biographical Record* 126 (1995): 35–45.

# Chapter 10

§

---

# GERMAN CHURCHES: REFORMED AND SECTARIAN

### Church of the Brethren, German Reformed and Evangelical Synod, Moravian, Schwenkfelder, United Brethren in Christ and Evangelical Association

---

## QUICK STATS

### FIRST ARRIVED IN THE U.S.:
Early 1700s

### DOMINANT REGIONS:
mid-Atlantic, New York, Virginia, North Carolina, Midwest, California

### DOMINANT ETHNIC ORIGIN:
German

### AFFILIATED FAITHS:
See affiliated faiths of individual denominations below

This chapter covers the German Reformed Church and several other German denominations, including (among others) Church of the Brethren, German Reformed and Evangelical Synod, Moravian, and Schwenkfelder. Entries below include brief historical background and a general description of records and where to find them.

Determining the church affiliations of German ancestors in the United States can be tricky. As a body, German immigrants were some of the most religiously diverse. Large numbers were Jewish, Catholic, or Lutheran.

Further complicating the historical picture, Germans from various religious traditions often settled in the same locales. For example, in the 1800s Berks County, Pennsylvania, had Germans who were Lutheran, Baptist, Catholic, Reformed, Mennonite, Amish, United Brethren in Christ,

Moravian, Church of the Brethren, members of splinter groups of these faiths, and more.[1] This much diversity in a single county makes it difficult to guess your German ancestors' faith solely based on where they lived, as may sometimes be possible for other immigrant groups.

Also noteworthy is the fact that multiple German-language churches (not all named here) included "Brethren" in their titles. It may take some time to identify your ancestors' German church. Read carefully the names of churches and note their locations, pastors' names, and any other details that might help you distinguish them from one another.

A few of the faiths named below are described as Anabaptist. Common within Anabaptist faiths was the practice of adult or "believer" baptism as opposed to infant baptism. Knowing that an ancestor belonged to an Anabaptist church may help you a) look for his or her baptismal records in the right season of life; b) better understand an ancestor's beliefs; and c) locate church records, particularly as family members may have moved from one Anabaptist church to another. If your family belonged to an Anabaptist faith, the Anabaptist Chronology Chart by Richard Cryer, available from Masthof Publishers (https://www.masthof.com), could prove tremendously helpful. (See also Chapter 13.)

Several German churches did practice infant baptism. This practice has been described earlier in the book, but it's worth noting that in many German churches, the tradition of naming sponsors or godparents was especially important. Whether godparents were relatives, close friends, or prominent community members, they often played a major role in helping to raise a child, especially if a parent died prematurely.

Many ethnic German church records in the United States were written in German, using old German Gothic script or printed in the Fraktur typeface. These guides are especially recommended:

- *If I Can, You Can: Decipher Germanic Records,* by Edna M Bentz (San Diego: E.M. Bentz, 1982). This older resource has plenty of word lists, including illnesses, occupations, and other terms that may appear in German records.

- *Deciphering Handwriting in German Documents,* 2nd ed., by Roger Minert (Provo, Utah: GRT Publications, 2013). Geared for German records in general, this book also applies to German-language church records. It offers plenty of word lists, script examples, and other useful resources.

- *The Family Tree German Genealogy Guide,* by James M. Beidler (Cincinnati: Family Tree Books, 2014), contains translation tips, an introduction to church records in Germany, and other helpful information.

- For a beginner's German research page with links to German handwriting aids and word lists, go to the FamilySearch wiki home page (https://www.familysearch.org/wiki), enter "Germany" in the search box, and click on the Getting Started page.

- Find an excellent tutorial for Old German Gothic script at http://www.suetterlinschrift.de/ Englisch/Sutterlin.htm. This site allows users to enter known words (such as family names) to see what they look like in Old German Gothic script, or Suetterlin.

In addition, it may be helpful to search among regional religious record collections. For example, *German Churches of Metropolitan New York: A Research Guide,* by Richard Haberstroh, CG (New York: New York Genealogical & Biographical Society, 2000), can help your New York research, as might church records available through the New York Genealogical & Biographical Society (read a helpful article at https://newyorkgenealogy.org/church). The German Genealogy Group (http://www.germangenealogygroup.com/) has databases for both New York German church records and St. Louis church baptisms and marriages. In Cincinnati, another destination for Ger-

---

1   Richard Frank Wennell, "Churches: The Churches of Berks County," *Pennsylvania USGenWeb Archives*, http://files.usgwarchives. net/pa/berks/church/list.txt. Accessed 7 Dec 2018.

man immigrants, the Hamilton County Genealogical Society (https://hcgsohio.org/) has identified, indexed, and published many local church records; explore its website for additional resources.

## CHURCH OF THE BRETHREN (GERMAN BAPTIST BRETHREN, "DUNKARDS")

The Church of the Brethren is the largest of several denominations that trace their 1708 origins to Schwarzenau, Germany. Theologically, they are part of the Anabaptist tradition. In the United States, the Church of the Brethren (http://www.brethren.org/) had the strongest presence in Pennsylvania, Virginia, Ohio, Indiana, Illinois, and California. Congregations practice "believer baptism" (rather than infant baptism) and observe a Love Feast communion service that includes feetwashing and a common meal.[2] Throughout most of the 18th and 19th centuries, Brethren were commonly known as "Dunkards," or "Dunkers," for their unique baptismal practice of immersing three times. Brethren have sometimes been confused with other, unrelated groups, such as the United Brethren, United Brethren in Christ (see below), and the Brethren in Christ (https://bicus.org).

Within the Schwarzenau tradition are also the Brethren Church (https://www.brethrenchurch.org/); Conservative Grace Brethren Churches, International (https://www.cgbci.org); Charis Fellowship (formerly, National Fellowship of Grace Brethren Churches, https://charisfellowship.us); the Dunkard Brethren Church (http://www.dunkardbrethrenchurch.com); the Old German Baptist Brethren ("Old Order Brethren"); and the Old Order German Baptist Brethren, New Conference (http://www.ogbbc.org).

Original church records for baptisms and marriages prior to the late 19th century for Brethren congregations are virtually nonexistent. Many older congregations, however, often maintained a graveyard near or next to the meetinghouse; burial records may exist. Records that do exist tend to be genealogically sparse. For example, women's maiden names may be omitted, or members may be referred to by their initials rather than given names.

Congregations generally maintain their own records, so start your search with the congregation locator tool on the main church website (http://www.brethren.org/, "Find a church"). *The Brethren Encyclopedia* (4 vols.) offers basic information on all congregations, biographies of key Brethren leaders, articles on dozens of prominent Brethren families, and extensive lists of ministers and missionaries.

The Brethren Historical Library and Archives (BHLA, http://www.brethren.org/bhla/) in Elgin, Illinois, keeps files on almost every congregation, which may include directories and other historical materials. It is the official repository for Brethren congregational records, and it actively collects genealogical information on Brethren families. Their collections of *Gospel Messenger* and other church newsletters contain marriage notices and obituaries or death notices for many prominent members and church leaders. In addition, library staff can consult *Brethren Encyclopedia* entries on specific congregations (which may include lists of founding members) as well as lists of ordained ministers and missionaries.

The BHLA website also has

- an excellent bibliography on the history of the Brethren, a list of repositories with Brethren collections, and some resources on the other Brethren churches;
- a link to search many of their manuscript finding aids in ArchiveGrid; and

2  Email from David Eller, Editor, *Brethren Roots*, 12 February 2019.

- the Brethren Digital Archives, a growing online collection for all Brethren periodicals (many of them containing obituaries and other genealogical information).

The Brethren Heritage Center in Brookville, Ohio (http://www.brethrenheritagecenter.org/), is an independent research center and museum that collects genealogical information on all Schwarzenau Brethren groups. It is particularly strong on Old Order churches in Ohio.

The Fellowship of Brethren Genealogists (https://www.cob-net.org/fobg/) "foster[s] communication among persons tracing the same Brethren ancestral lines and encourage[s] research in Brethren genealogy." The group claims more than 200 members, who share information, tips, and encouragement via a family surname directory of more than 4,000 surnames. The quarterly newsletter, *Brethren Roots*, comes with membership; back issues are searchable in PERSI (see Chapter 3 for more on PERSI).

## GERMAN REFORMED AND THE EVANGELICAL SYNOD

The presence of German Reformed Church members in the colonial U.S. dates to the early 1700s. Many German and German-Swiss emigrated to escape the ongoing political, religious, and economic fallout of the Thirty Years War. Some were wealthy enough to pay their own passage; many sold their labor as indentured servants. Most came to Pennsylvania, New York, and the mid-Atlantic region.

In the early years, German Reformed ministers were in short supply in the colonies. The Dutch Reformed Church helped fill the gap; the ministers it sent were primarily German. A Coetus or synod of the various German Reformed leaders in the colonies was officially sanctioned in 1747.

"In addition to the ties with the Dutch Reformed, the German Reformed also established close ties with the German Lutherans. These two groups shared a common language and common culture. Because they also shared many of the same problems in the colonies, they quickly formed union churches in the early 18th century, sharing the cost and use of a building, each congregation worshiping on alternate Sundays. There are still a few of these union churches today. The record books of many churches contain records of both Reformed and Lutheran baptisms, marriages, deaths, and confirmations."[3]

After the Revolutionary War, the Synod of the German Reformed Church in the United States of America was formed, with 178 German-language congregations and an estimated 40,000 adherents (about 13,000 of whom were communicants, or full-fledged members).[4] Throughout the early 1800s, many Reformed members and clergy were influenced by doctrinal controversies and the missionary enthusiasm of other German sects, resulting in a splintering of the Reformed Synod (though all independent synods that formed between the 1840s and 1870s eventually rejoined the Reformed Synod). The Reformed Synod was renamed the Reformed Church in the United States in 1863.

The future of the German Reformed Church lay in union with the Evangelical Synod of North America, which has its own history. "The Evangelical Synod of North America grew out of the Evangelical Church in Germany, which had been formed by the union of Reformed and Lutheran churches in 1817 . . . . People and clergy from these newly formed Evangelical churches immigrated to the United States, settling primarily in the Midwest. Most of these churches remained independent until formed into the Kirchenverein des Westens [the German Evangelical Church Society of the West] in 1840. Other groups of Evangelical churches continued to join the Kirchenverein during the 19th century and it changed its name to the Evangelical Synod of North

---

3  Email from Reverend Richard R. Berg, Evangelical & Reformed Historical Society Board President and Archivist Emeritus, 28 January 2019.
4  Sydney E. Ahlstrom, *A Religious History of the American People* (New Haven: Yale University Press, 1972), 250.

America. So, although some Reformed and Lutheran churches joined the Evangelical Synod, it was really already a union of Reformed and Lutheran churches in Germany."[5]

In 1934 the Evangelical Synod of North America merged with the Reformed Church in the United States. The resulting Evangelical and Reformed Church itself united with the Congregational Christian Churches in 1957 to form the United Church of Christ.

Reformed and Evangelical church record collections may contain a variety of records:

- Membership lists may exist, occasionally even sorted by family, with the names of family members, when they joined the church, and perhaps a previous residence.

- Baptismal records may have included the person's age or birth date, baptismal date, name of at least one parent, and names of sponsors and witnesses. Humphrey writes that for the Reformed Church, "infants are the proper subjects of baptism. . . . The Reformed Church limited baptism to children or infants of communicant members; one or both parents had to have received confirmation in the church."[6]

- Confirmations often included only the date, as part of a list.

- Marriage records often had only basic information (bride/groom names, date of wedding, and officiant).

- Death and/or burial records may have included the deceased's name, a relative's name and relationship, age at death, cause of death, death and burial dates, and occasionally an additional detail such as a maiden name or birthplace.

Additional congregational records may include histories, minutes of the consistory (church governing body), communicant lists, lists of elders and deacons, financial records, and more.

Today, the United Church of Christ Archives does not maintain congregational records of its predecessor churches. Other archives exist for that purpose, if the individual church doesn't have its own records (and some records have been published).

- The Evangelical and Reformed Historical Society in Pennsylvania (http://erhs.info/) archives records from both of its founding churches, including original and transcribed church records; "minutes of synods, classes, congregations; records of the mission boards; hymnals; liturgies, and important publications such as the *Reformed Church Messenger* and the *Mercersburg Review*."[7] The society website has a searchable catalog; search specifically among larger collections of church records at http://erhs.info/home/resources/erhs-church-records. It holds collections pertaining to over 800 individual churches. Some have been transcribed and translated from German; others have not.

- The Evangelical Synod Archives in Missouri (https://www.eden.edu/the-archives-at-eden-theological-seminary/) maintains basic files on most pastors and congregations with roots in that faith tradition. Its website states that congregation history files "typically include written histories, membership directories and other materials of general historical interest." The archives also has many church records, especially records from St. Louis, Missouri, and the surrounding area. However, according to its website, "Most church records held by the archives have been microfilmed and are available for research at the St. Louis County Library History and Genealogy Department. . . . The library staff will also do lookups. . . . Please provide the name of the person, the name of the church, and the specific record you are looking for. Church records usually include baptisms, confirmations, marriages, and deaths. The Archives accepts requests for lookups in church records not held by St. Louis County Library."

5   Berg email, 2019.
6   Humphrey, *Baptismal Records*, 52.
7   "About Us," *Evangelical & Reformed Historical Society* website, http://erhs.info/home/about-us/.

## MORAVIAN (UNITY OF BRETHREN)

The modern Moravian Church, also known as Unitas Fratrum or Unity of Brethren, traces its origins to followers of martyr Jan Hus (1369–1415); it was organized in 1457 and became one of the earliest Protestant religious communities. Moravians experienced severe persecution and dispersion during the Counter-Reformation before finding sanctuary on the Saxony estate of Count Nikolaus Ludwig von Zinzendorf (1700–1760) in modern-day Germany in 1722. From there, Moravians began a worldwide missionary outreach to the unchurched among native peoples and the enslaved.

In 1735 a group of Moravians settled in the colony of Georgia, but eventually made its way to the Lehigh Valley, Pennsylvania. Semi-communal settlements grew up in Nazareth and Bethlehem, Pennsylvania, and in the Wachovia tract near present-day Winston-Salem, North Carolina. Moravians eventually owned nearly 100,000 acres in what is now Forsyth County. Congregations were also founded in Philadelphia and Staten Island, and missions targeting Native Americans spread from Maine south to Georgia.

German and Scandinavian immigration expanded membership into the upper Midwest in the late 1800s. But the Moravians never gained large numbers of adherents, and their membership remained concentrated in Pennsylvania and North Carolina.

Moravian records can be genealogically rich. Family registers may group together entire families, with names, birth dates and places of parents and each child, and sometimes baptismal and/or confirmation dates. Registers for early immigrant groups may include actual dates of arrival.

The social structure of Moravian communities was unique and led to some distinctive records. Parents kept their babies for 18 months, when the toddlers joined a progressive series of "choirs" or peer groups that were stratified by age and gender. Those under age 4 were in a nursery. Children were sent to the little boys' or little girls' choirs (age 4–11), then to the older boys' or older girls' choirs (age 12–18). At age 19, members joined choirs for single men ("brethren") or women ("sisters") until they married and joined the married people's choir. Individuals may be identified in records as "Brother" or "Sister" to express their sense of religious community.

Choir lists often include extensive genealogical data. "For a married person there is given name, date and place of birth, ancestral denominational stock . . ., date and place of joining a Moravian congregation, date and place of first communion, date and place of marriage, number of sons and daughters; and the page supplies an additional column in which occupation, church office or other important item, may be entered. In the case of a widow the date of death of the husband is often given; the maiden name of married women and widows is noted. For children the name of the father is often inserted in brackets if there were two or more families of the same last name in the congregation."[8]

Infants were baptized immediately after birth, and baptismal records may include dates of birth and baptism, parents' names (including maiden surnames), sponsors' names, the officiant's name, and possibly later remarks about confirmation or moving out of the church. Several sponsors could be listed, and at least in earlier years, sponsors were the same gender as the baptized child.

Marriage records may have names, dates of birth, and parents' names, along with the marriage date. Death and/or burial records may include the date, place and cause of death, burial place, funeral date and text, parents' names (for deceased children), and even a short biographical sketch.

Among the most valuable Moravian records are the *Lebensläufe*, or memoirs, in which members wrote their own life stories. As described by Fries, "The Memoir is a biographical sketch, some-

8   Adelaide L. Fries, "Moravian Church Records as a Source of Genealogical Material," *National Genealogical Society Quarterly* 24:1 (March 1936), 5.

times autobiographical in its major portion, but usually prepared by the pastor of the congregation, with some assistance from the family, and with careful search of the Church registers for dates. In the earlier days it was often read at a service soon after the burial; today the Memoir is read in conjunction with the funeral service. Naturally some of the Memoirs have been lost during the years, but there are many on file, and when one can be found it gives the life-story in detail, carefully including the religious experiences of the member."[9]

Moravian community diaries are another unusual genealogical resource. "Community diaries were written daily and shared with other communities so that each could be informed of the news of that community. Baptisms of Native Americans, travelers who stopped by (including non-Moravians), the health of their members, and expected immigrant parties were all part of the news shared by the community to their brethren. They named names (including name changes for converted Native Americans) and give insights into the daily news. Some communities and chroniclers were better than others, but do look for the community diaries in the area your ancestor lived. Although he may not have been Moravian, perhaps he had dealings with them. The Moravians . . . welcomed all travelers and visitors. They often took in non-Moravian family members to care for and subsequently bury in their cemeteries. The Bethlehem Diary, from 1742 to 1871, contains 33,352 manuscript pages, only some of which have been published. . . . The Records of the Moravian Church in North Carolina, 1752–1876, are published in 13 volumes."[10]

Some of these resources are now available online. The Bethlehem Digital History Project (http://bdhp.moravian.edu/) includes images and translations for the Bethlehem area community diary (1742–63); meeting minutes; choir catalogs and diaries; registers of marriages, baptisms, and deaths; visitors' accounts; and more.

Ministers' diaries, account books, correspondence, conference minute books, travel diaries, and other records may also exist; ask for these wherever you search for Moravian records. Records may have been written in German or old script German. The latter requires special training to read; see the resources at the beginning of this chapter. Minute books and diaries may give special insight into an ancestor's military service (or lack of it), as many Moravians were conscientious objectors; they considered themselves part of a transnational community that owed allegiance to God and not to any country.[11] Trace Moravians also through land records and wills available at local courthouses.

The Moravian Church in North America has a list and map of active congregations on its website (https://www.moravian.org). Contact congregations to ask about old congregation records or search online for published records. Then contact the correct provincial archive to see what additional records they have:

- The Northern Province Archives (https://www.moravianchurcharchives.org/), in Bethlehem, Pennsylvania, collects materials for all of the United States except North Carolina, Florida, Georgia, and Virginia. Search its holdings and the Moravian Roots genealogy database, which contains information from a growing number of baptismal, marriage, removal, funeral, and other records that have been indexed from the archive's collections. Find an inventory of church registers in its collection at http://www.moravianchurcharchives.org/documents/ChReg.pdf. The website also contains a helpful page of links to other resources on Moravian history in the U.S.

- The Southern Province Archives (http://moravianarchives.org/) in Winston-Salem, North Carolina, collects Moravian materials for the Carolinas, Florida, Georgia, and Virginia. See

---

9   Ibid., 6.
10  Email from Elissa Scalise Powell, CG, CGL, 9 February 2019.
11  Email from J. Eric Elliott, Archivist, Moravian Archives, 8 February 2019.

the website for a description of its manuscript, photograph, map, and other collections, which include more than 14,000 memoirs. Many of its records have been published in a series, *Records of the Moravians in North Carolina*, which is indexed; an online version is available on the website. Contact the archive for a lookup, or locate the series at a major research library near you.

Don't neglect the collections of societies, archives, and libraries near where Moravian ancestors lived. For example, the Wachovia Historical Society (http://www.wachoviahistoricalsociety.org) in Winston-Salem, North Carolina, is dedicated to preserving the story of the Moravian Church in the South. See its website for a list of publications and a description of its holdings.

A final tip for researchers: though the faith originated in Moravia, few Moravian immigrants were actually born there. They more likely came from Germany, Denmark, Sweden, Switzerland, Holland, or England;[12] Moravian records may point to their overseas birthplaces.

## SCHWENKFELDERS

Between 1731 and 1737, more than 200 followers of Silesian nobleman Caspar Schwenckfeld von Ossig (1489–1561) arrived in Philadelphia, fleeing religious persecution. They came in six migrations—the largest group of 180 coming in 1734—and settled in Montgomery, Berks, Bucks, and Lehigh counties in Pennsylvania. In 1782 they formed the Society of the Schwenkfelders.

Though not forbidden, baptism and communion were not practiced until the 1890s, when communion was begun, so you will find few if any such records.[13] Infants were "prayed over" in early years, but through the 20th century, the practice was modified to either consecrating or baptizing of infants, depending on the congregation. Church membership, marriage, adult baptism, and clergy records were not kept until the start of the 20th century.

However, tracing genealogy has been a common practice in Schwenkfelder families, who prize their affiliation with the original group of immigrants. According to one researcher, "From the very beginning of their arrival they kept meticulous records of the births, marriages and deaths of their members. They also maintained diaries which contain voluminous information concerning their activities."[14] In 1923 *The Genealogical Record of the Schwenkfelder Families* was published. An imaged, indexed version is on Ancestry (http://search.ancestry.com/search/db.aspx?dbid=26138). Another helpful resource is *The Schwenkfelders in Pennsylvania*, by H.W. Kriebel, published in 1904.

The Schwenkfelder Library & Heritage Center (http://www.schwenkfelder.com/) collects all historical materials relating to the Schwenkfelders and the Perkiomen Valley. Among them are the older records of many congregations, including membership records, minutes, financial records, and pastors' and school records. The Society of the Descendants of the Schwenkfeldian Exiles (https://schwenkfelderexilesociety.org/) meets annually at the Heritage Center and maintains an update of the 1923 *Genealogical Record*. The website has lists of immigrants organized by ship arrival and cemetery information.

## UNITED BRETHREN IN CHRIST AND EVANGELICAL ASSOCIATION

The United Brethren in Christ has its roots in the intermingled German Reformed, Mennonite, and Methodist experiences. Mennonite pastor Martin Boehm and Reformed pastor William Otterbein met in Lancaster, Pennsylvania, in 1767 and began a movement that spread through the

---

12    Fries, 1.

13    "The Schwenkfelders," *United Church of Christ* website, http://www.ucc.org/about-us_hidden-histories_the-schwenkfelders.

14    Milton Rubincam. "In Search of Pennsylvania Germans: Sources for Family History," in *World Conference on Records: Preserving Our Heritage*, series 342. Salt Lake City: Church of Jesus Christ of Latter-day Saints, 1980, p. 4.

German-language churches in Pennsylvania, Maryland, and Virginia. They formed as the Church of the United Brethren in Christ at their first official general conference in 1800.

For many years, circuit-riding preachers served United Brethren groups as their influence pressed westward with German migration into Ohio, Indiana, and Illinois. In 1889 theological and administrative differences led a sizeable group to splinter from the main body. Both groups kept the same name, the smaller branch referred to as "Radicals" or "Old Constitution" (because of their continuing support for the church's original constitution) and the larger body as "Liberals" or "New Constitution."

In 1946 the New Constitution branch merged with the Evangelical Association, which had begun in 1803 as a Methodist-influenced German church in eastern Pennsylvania and gradually spread into Ohio. The resulting denomination, named the Evangelical United Brethren Church, itself merged with the Methodist Church in 1968 to become part of the United Methodist Church. The smaller branch continues today as Church of the United Brethren in Christ, USA (http://ub.org/), headquartered in Huntington, Indiana.

Original church membership records, with lists of church members, may include details about the person's admission and dismission. Separate lists may appear for baptisms of adults or children, marriages, deaths, and/or funerals. Details vary but often at least include the date of the event and officiant. Church minutes may contain additional details about individuals and the church community.

The United Brethren Historical Center (UBHC) at Huntington University in Indiana (https://www.huntington.edu/united-brethren-historical-center/) houses the Archives of the Church of the United Brethren in Christ and the United Brethren Historical Society. The Center keeps information relating to congregations of the original, undivided church (1800–1889) and today's Church of the United Brethren in Christ (1889–present). The annual *Yearbook of the United Brethren in Christ* can help identify congregations and pastors. However, data on everyday members in the 1800s is sparse, as much of that information followed the New Constitution church (they mostly have information relating to ministers, and continue to add to this information by indexing obituaries). The UBHC collects information on ministers, missionaries, and lay people, and maintains obituary, wedding, and biography files with records from church publications. The Center encourages researchers to contact its staff for assistance in determining which denomination is relevant to their ancestors.

Those researching ancestors who were members of the "New Constitution" church (1889–1946), the Evangelical Association, and/or the Evangelical United Brethren Church should see the chapter on Methodists. The Historical Society of the United Methodist Church maintains records on these church bodies, as they eventually merged into this denomination. *History of the Church of the United Brethren in Christ,* by A.W. Drury, can be read online at Internet Archive (https://archive.org/details/UBwmHistoryOfTheChurchOfTheUBCByAWDrury/page/n4). Individual church membership records or histories of these churches may now be in Methodist conference archives; also consult "Guide to the Records of the Church of the United Brethren in Christ Annual Conferences and Local Churches, 1810–1946," prepared by the General Commission on Archives and History of the United Methodist Church and available online at http://catalog.gcah.org/publicdata/gcah3985.pdf.

## FURTHER READING

Beidler, James M. *The Family Tree German Genealogy Guide*. Cincinnati: Family Tree Books, 2014.

Beidler, James M. *Trace Your German Roots Online: A Complete Guide to German Genealogy Websites*. Cincinnati: Family Tree Books, 2014.

Durnbaugh, Donald F. "Pennsylvania's Crazy Quilt of German Religious Groups," *Pennsylvania History* 68:8–30 (Winter 2001).

Fries, Adelaide L. "Moravian Church Records as a Source of Genealogical Material," *National Genealogical Society Quarterly* 24:1 (March 1936), 1–9.

Humphrey, John T. *Understanding and Using Baptismal Records*. Humphrey Publications, 1996.

Joyner, Peggy S. *Extant German Church Records from Virginia and West Virginia: A Checklist*. Baltimore, Md.: Society for the History of the Germans in Maryland, 1982.-

Meynen, Emil, comp. and ed. *Bibliography on the Colonial Germans of North America*. Baltimore, Md.: Genealogical Publishing Company, 1982.

Minert, Roger P. *German Immigrants in American Church Records* series. Rockland, Me.: Picton Press, 2006–15, 18 vols., and Orting, Wash.: Family Roots Publishing, 2016–18, 7 vols. These include abstracts from records of many different Protestant churches in Indiana, Wisconsin, Nebraska, Iowa, Illinois, Minnesota, South Dakota, North Dakota, Missouri, and Ohio.

*Pennsylvania German Church Records of Births, Baptisms, Marriages, Burials, etc. from the Pennsylvania German Society Proceedings and Addresses*, with an introduction by Don Yoder. 3 vols. Baltimore: Genealogical Publishing Company, 1983; reprinted 2009.

Powell, Elissa Scalise, CG, CGL. "Moravian Trails and Records," NGS Audio Recordings, 2017 (https://www.playbackngs.com/7770-s419).

*Sources and Documents* series of publications by the Pennsylvania German Society (http://www.pgs.org/documents.asp).

# Chapter 11

---

# LATTER-DAY SAINT (MORMON)

---

### *QUICK STATS*

### *CHURCH ORGANIZED IN THE U.S.:*
1830

### *DOMINANT REGIONS:*
Utah, Idaho, Nevada, California, Washington, Arizona, Wyoming

### *DOMINANT ETHNIC GROUPS:*
English, Danish, Norwegian

### *AFFILIATED FAITHS:*
Community of Christ (formerly The Reorganized Church of Jesus Christ
of Latter Day Saints)

## BACKGROUND

The Church of Jesus Christ of Latter-day Saints was founded in 1830 in New York by Joseph Smith. Thanks to traveling missionaries, the faith spread quickly throughout the Great Lakes region on both sides of the U.S.-Canada border and to England.

Throughout the 1800s, many converts migrated to a central gathering place. The first significant gathering place was Kirtland (1831–1838), a town in northeast Ohio. During that time period, church members also settled in parts of Jackson, Clay, and Caldwell counties in Missouri. After leaving both states under trying circumstances, the church built a planned city and new headquarters in Nauvoo, Illinois (1839–1846), to which thousands of converts flocked.

After Smith was killed in 1844, the largest group remained members of The Church of Jesus Christ of Latter-day Saints and are today commonly nicknamed Latter-day Saints or Mormons. This group migrated to the Utah wilderness along what became known as the Mormon Trail. During the exodus, the federal government recruited a military unit from among them to serve in the Mexican–American War, a unit called the Mormon Battalion.

Latter-day Saint settlers colonized the Intermountain West and parts of Mexico and Canada. Missionary efforts expanded in the United States, England, the South Pacific, Denmark, and elsewhere. About 90,000 British, Irish, Scandinavian, German, and other immigrants who joined the Church migrated to Utah, aided by rail service (beginning in 1869) and the Church's immigrant aid society, the Perpetual Emigrating Fund Company (1849–1887). In the 1890s, the Church stopped encouraging members to migrate to Utah. It has since continued to grow throughout the world and today numbers over 16 million members.

Not all who were members before 1844 stayed with the Utah-headquartered church. In 1860 Joseph Smith's son, Joseph Smith III, accepted leadership of the new Reorganized Church of Jesus Christ of Latter Day Saints (RLDS), which became strongest in the Midwest. It built communities in Lamoni, Iowa, and Independence, Missouri, where the faith is still headquartered. In 2001 the RLDS church was renamed Community of Christ; today it claims about a quarter million members. Other churches that share historical roots with The Church of Jesus Christ of Latter-day Saints have also formed. See a denominational tree at https://tinyurl.com/LDSdenomtree.

## ABOUT CONGREGATIONAL RECORDS

The following explanation applies specifically to The Church of Jesus Christ of Latter-day Saints; see below for a brief description of RLDS/Community of Christ records.

Membership records can be genealogically rich, though some have been lost and extant ones may vary in form and content. Few membership records exist for U.S. congregations before the 1850s. Membership records may include details pertaining to the following:

*Vital events and relationships.* These records may include birthdates and ages; marriage dates; and names of parents, spouses, and children.

*Baptisms and confirmations.* These two rites officially confer church membership and are generally performed in immediate sequence or within a short time of each other. Infant baptisms are not performed; those seeking baptism must be at least eight years old.

*Priesthood ordinations.* All males are encouraged to qualify by belief and conduct standards for ordination to various priesthood offices, though ordination was not available to men of African descent before 1978. Priesthood offices fall into two categories: the Aaronic (deacon, teacher, and priest) and the Melchizedek (elder, high priest, and another office known as "seventy," referencing the seventy disciples mentioned in Luke 10:1 in the New Testament). Men who served in specific church capacities may also have been ordained to special offices, such as bishop.

*Marriages.* Faithful adherents aspire to wed in a temple, where a ceremony known as a sealing binds a couple for both mortality and the afterlife. (Couples who have already wed civilly may still receive a sealing ceremony later.) Two more categories of weddings may be found in records: civil marriages and "church civil" weddings performed by church authorities, but not in a temple. Because of the practice of polygamy, officially sanctioned until 1890, you may find concurrent marriages for Latter-day Saint men. Church membership records before the 1900s generally do not have information about marriages, although separate lists of marriages performed by a bishop may exist.

## HOW TO FIND AND ACCESS MEMBERSHIP RECORDS

Latter-day Saints were generally given certificates for their own baptisms and confirmations, ordinations, and marriages. These may have been handed down in family collections.

Local congregations are called either "wards" or "branches" (the latter are smaller units), and each ward or branch belongs to regional bodies called "stakes." Wards and branches maintain records for current members. Stakes also keep some records, including histories. Regional missions, which oversee missionary work, generally predate the presence of congregations in a locale and may also have kept important records and histories.

Extant historical ward and stake records are archived in Salt Lake City at the Church History Library (CHL; go to https://history.ChurchofJesusChrist.org, click on the Visit tab and then select "Church History Library" from the dropdown list), which is distinct from the Family History Library (FHL; https://www.familysearch.org/wiki/en/Family_History_Library), also owned by the denomination. The CHL website has an extensive catalog and a series of guides to tracing Latter-day Saint roots, as well as an introduction to the many digitized resources on its site. Consider this an essential starting point! Some resources at the CHL, including membership records, are also available on microfilm at the FHL.

Locating ward membership records requires knowing the name of the person's ward or branch. Congregations generally take their names from the town. However, locales with large Latter-day Saint populations were home to many wards and stakes, which may have changed their boundaries and names over the years. Few maps exist of historical ward and stake boundaries.

You may find the name of a ward in a member's obituary. Andrew Jensen's *Encyclopedic History of the Church*, digitized online at https://lib.byu.edu/collections/miscellaneous-books/, describes many ward boundaries up until about 1940 in entries on specific wards or branches, stakes, and missions. The 1967 guide *Alphabetical Index to Ward and Branch Organization*, available at the FHL, may prove helpful too.

If you can identify the stake, you may be able to locate a stake history, which should mention the names of its wards and perhaps enough information on ward boundaries or ward members' names that you could identify the ward. Wards in different stakes might have the same names; for example, Springfield Ward in Ohio and Virginia.

The Early Church Information file, searchable at https://familysearch.org, documents more than 1.5 million members since the 1830s. Entries may include genealogical and biographical data, church membership information, and bibliographic sources. The fifty-volume *Membership of The Church of Jesus Christ of Latter-day Saints, 1830–1848*, by Susan Easton Black—an excellent starting place for identifying early adherents—is searchable at Ancestry (https://www.ancestry.com/). An overlapping resource is the LDS Member Name Index, 1830–1845, also at Ancestry. The Deceased Member Records (1941–1988) collection at the CHL provides helpful genealogical information for 20th-century members.

## OTHER RECORDS OF INTEREST

*Autobiographies and biographies.* First-person life writings such as diaries and autobiographies may exist; Latter-day Saint tradition encourages personal history writing. Many have been collected by the CHL, Brigham Young University (BYU) Library's Special Collections (https://lib.byu.edu/special-collections/), and other regional or private archives, including

- Utah State University (https://archives.usu.edu/);
- Weber State University (for Weber and Davis counties and the city of Ogden; https://library.weber.edu/collections/special_collections);
- The University of Utah (https://www.lib.utah.edu/collections/special-collections/);
- International Society Daughters of Utah Pioneers (http://www.dupinternational.org/);
- Utah State Historical Society (https://history.utah.gov/utah-state-historical-society/); and
- Southern Utah University (https://contentdm.li.suu.edu/digital/).

Look for writings by neighbors and associates of your relatives, as well as your own kin. A database called Mormons and Their Neighbors (https://lib.byu.edu/collections/mormons-and-their-neighbors/) indexes over 100,000 life sketches from the Intermountain West.

Many compiled biographies of early Latter-day Saints have been published. A directory on the FamilySearch Research Wiki (https://www.familysearch.org/wiki/en/LDS_Biography) may not be completely updated with links to digitized versions; search Google to find copies online.

*Missionary service.* A significant number of men—and since the mid-1900s, a growing number of women—have participated in full-time volunteer missionary work both in the United States and abroad. The Early Mormon Missionaries 1830–1930 database at https://history.ChurchofJesus Christ.org (click on the Research tab and then select "Early Mormon Missionaries" from the dropdown list) is free to search. Entries may include the missionary's birth and death information, parents' names, dates and places of service, and links to digitized missionary registers, diaries, correspondence, or other materials. A collection of digitized missionary diaries (https://lib. byu.edu/collections/mormon-missionary-diaries/) is browsable by region as well as surname in various times and places.

*Patriarchal blessings.* Patriarchal blessings, given verbally but documented in writing, are considered God's counsel for an individual's life course. These confidential documents are available only to direct-line descendants who are current members of The Church of Jesus Christ of Latter-day Saints; they may request and view copies at https://ChurchofJesusChrist.org (log in and select Patriarchal Blessings under the main menu).

*Military Records.* The Nauvoo Legion was a city militia chartered in 1840 as part of the Illinois state militia. Almost all enlistees were Latter-day Saints. Search a list of Nauvoo Legion members on Ancestry's website. Original records of the Utah Territorial Militia, which was still referred to as the Nauvoo Legion during the early Utah years, are at the CHL and Utah State Archives. FamilySearch has published "Utah, Territorial Militia Records, 1849–1877" (https://www.family search.org/search/collection/1462415), a collection of "muster rolls, correspondence, payrolls, morning reports, receipts, returns, and journals" from the Utah State Archives.

The Mormon Battalion, previously mentioned, was a separate military unit. An index to Mormon Battalion pension applications is at FamilySearch (https://www.familysearch.org/search/collection/1852758); originals are at the National Archives and Records Administration (https://www.archives.gov/). The Mormon Battalion Association (http://www.mormonbattalion.com/) documents the lives and activities of this unit and may prove a helpful resource. See an online history of Latter-day Saint participation in the Civil War in the Further Readings section below.

*Migration and immigration.* Start with these easily accessible and searchable web resources that contain compiled lists of Latter-day Saint traveling companies, along with records pertaining to those groups:

- Mormon Migration (https://mormonmigration.lib.byu.edu/), with compiled immigrant passenger lists, ship names, and first-person overseas travel accounts for specific journeys;
- Mormon Pioneer Overland Travel (https://history.ChurchofJesusChrist.org; click on the Research tab and then select "Mormon Pioneer Overland Travel" from the dropdown list), a database of overland domestic travelers, with related trail diaries and other historical accounts.

Immigrants who traveled to the United States may also appear in mainstream passenger and departure lists: most European Latter-day Saint converts departed through Liverpool. Emigration records kept by the Scandinavian, British, and Netherlands missions are on microfilm at the FHL and CHL. Databases of emigrants from Norway (1886–1900) and Denmark (1872–1894) are searchable at American Ancestors (https://www.americanancestors.org/).

The Perpetual Emigrating Fund Company kept debtor lists and other records. Research these at the FHL and CHL, and consult the compiled publication *Names of Persons and Sureties Indebted to the Perpetual Emigrating Fund Company from 1850 to 1877*, digitized at Internet Archive (https://archive.org/). The Immigrant Ancestors Project (http://immigrants.byu.edu/) and the Welsh Mormon Immigrant Project (http://welshmormon.byu.edu/) may prove helpful.

*Church censuses.* In 1852–1853, local bishops (ward leaders) in Utah created head-of-household censuses, available in print and on microfilm at the FHL and BYU. Between 1914 and 1960, periodic church-wide censuses captured rich genealogical data on individuals. Find these on microfilm at the CHL, FHL, and BYU.

*Local histories.* Search the card catalogs of the CHL, FHL, and BYU for manuscript and published histories of Latter-day Saint settlements, missions, wards or branches, and stakes. Additional resources are available for early communities where Church members gathered:

- Historic Kirtland (https://www.ChurchofJesusChrist.org/locations/historic-kirtland-visitors-center) is a historic attraction that tells the story of the Church in Kirtland. Visitors may search an on-site database of early members in Kirtland. See the Further Readings list below.

- Historic Nauvoo (https://www.historicnauvoo.net/) is a fully recreated 1840s village with more than thirty homes, businesses, and other buildings that interpret the Latter-day Saint story. The Historic Nauvoo Land and Records Office (https://www.historicnauvoo.net/land-and-records) has a database for Latter-day Saint residents (1839–1845). Ancestry has an 1842 Nauvoo tax list and Nauvoo-era marriages. The Joseph Smith Historic Site (https://www.cofchrist.org/visit-nauvoo) in Nauvoo tells the town's story from an RLDS/Community of Christ perspective. *Nauvoo & Hancock County, Illinois: A Guide to Family History and Historical Sources,* by Kip Sperry, is an additional resource.

- Winter Quarters, Nebraska, was a temporary home for many Latter-day Saints as they prepared for the westward trek. Learn more at Early Latter-day Saints: A Mormon Pioneer Database (http://earlylds.com/) and the Winter Quarters Project (http://winterquarters.byu.edu/).

*Family trees.* The FamilySearch website (https://familysearch.org) is owned by The Church of Jesus Christ of Latter-day Saints, which encourages its members for religious reasons to document their family trees. Thus, Latter-day Saint forebears are heavily represented on FamilySearch's Family Tree, a giant, unified family tree. After creating a free login at the site, select "Tree" under the Search tab to find ancestors who may already have profiles on the Family Tree. Additionally, thousands of Latter-day Saints have submitted individual trees that are now part of the Ancestral File and Pedigree Resource File collections, searchable by clicking on Search and then selecting "Genealogies."

*Lineage societies.* The Daughters of Utah Pioneers (http://www.dupinternational.org) has an online index to its files, which include thousands of biographical sketches and photos of early Utah Latter-day Saint pioneers. The National Society of the Sons of Utah Pioneers (https://www.sup1847.com/) has several indexes on Ancestry, including Pioneer Immigrants to Utah Territory.

The comprehensive *A Guide to Mormon Family History Sources,* by Kip Sperry (Provo, Utah: Ancestry Publishing, 2007), is highly recommended for further depth and breadth of coverage on tracing Latter-day Saint ancestors.

## RLDS/COMMUNITY OF CHRIST RECORDS

The Community of Christ Library and Archives (CCLA; https://www.cofchrist.org/visit-library-and-archives) in Independence, Missouri, houses some original handwritten individual membership record ledgers (1859–1922), which may include baptism, confirmation, ordination, migration, and expulsion details. Other archival holdings include local branch and jurisdictional records, diaries, autobiographies, correspondence, and oral histories. The CCLA hosts a monthly genealogy day; learn more and find links to additional resources at https://www.cofchrist.org/about-the-archives.

Additional resources may prove helpful in tracing RLDS roots. A Deceased Members Card File (1877–1995) is available on microfilm at the CCLA and FHL. Susan Easton Black's *Early Members of the Reorganized Church of Jesus Christ of Latter Day Saints* is available in several libraries and searchable at Ancestry; digitized volumes are available via the FamilySearch Catalog. See further readings for an article by Barbara Hands Bernauer on the Community of Christ archives.

## FURTHER READING

Alford, Kenneth L., ed. *Civil War Saints*. Provo, Utah: Religious Studies Center, Brigham Young University, 2012; also Salt Lake City: Deseret Book Company, 2012. Digitized version available online at https://rsc.byu.edu/award-winning/civil-war-saints.

Allen, James B., Ronald W. Walker, and David J. Whittaker. *Studies in Mormon History, 1830–1997: An Indexed Bibliography*. Urbana, Ill.: University of Illinois Press, 2000.

Arrington, Leonard J., and Davis Bitton. *The Mormon Experience: A History of the Latter-day Saints*. 2nd ed. Urbana, Ill.: University of Illinois Press, 1992.

Backman, Milton V., Jr. *A Profile of Latter-day Saints of Kirtland, Ohio and Members of Zion's Camp*. Provo, Utah: Brigham Young University, 1983.

Bernauer, Barbara Hands. "Community of Christ Archives: A Richard Howard Legacy," *The John Whitmer Historical Association Journal* 33:1 (Spring/Summer 2013), pp. 45–66.

Howlett, David J., Barbara B. Walden, and John C. Hamer. *Community of Christ: An Illustrated History*. Independence, Mo.: Herald Publishing House, 2010.

Larsen, Paul. *Crash Course in Family History: How to Discover Your Family Tree and Stories*. 5th ed. St. George, Utah: EasyFamilyHistory.com, 2014. This illustrated handbook is largely written for a Latter-day Saint audience.

Launius, Roger D. *Joseph Smith III: Pragmatic Prophet*. Urbana, Ill.: University of Illinois Press, 1985.

Shipps, Jan. *Mormonism: The Story of a New Religious Tradition*. Urbana, Ill.: University of Illinois Press, 1985.

Sperry, Kip. *Kirtland, Ohio: Guide to Family History and Historical Sources*. Provo, Utah: Brigham Young University, 2005.

Sperry, Kip. *Nauvoo & Hancock County, Illinois: A Guide to Family History and Historical Sources*. Provo, Utah: Religious Studies Center, Brigham Young University, 2014; also Salt Lake City: Deseret Book Company, 2014.

# *Chapter 12*

§

## LUTHERAN

### *QUICK STATS*

#### *FIRST ARRIVED IN THE U.S.:*
1637

#### *DOMINANT REGIONS:*
Eastern seaboard and Pennsylvania (colonial era), Midwest

#### *DOMINANT ETHNIC ORIGIN:*
German, Swedish, Dutch, Norwegian, Finnish

#### *AFFILIATED FAITHS:*
German Reformed

## BACKGROUND

American Lutheranism represents a diverse group of immigrants who arrived at different points in time and settled in different places. They often started their own congregations, called *parishes* (though up until the mid-1900s, a single pastor might have served multiple congregations and his assignment would still have been called a parish). Over time, some parishes formed or participated in regional governing bodies known as synods, but loyalties could and did change. By the mid-1800s, there were 250 independent Lutheran organizations in the U.S. Many of these groups eventually merged into the few major Lutheran bodies of today.

Swedish and Dutch settlers founded the first Lutheran congregations in the future United States in the 1630s and 1640s. But Germans and a wider group of Scandinavian immigrants can claim credit for much of the growth of Lutheranism in this country.

In the early 1700s, thousands of Palatine Germans established a string of Lutheran churches in the areas they settled, from New Jersey up the Hudson River to Albany. Their presence helped support the next generation of German Lutherans, who went instead to Pennsylvania and migrated south and west from there. By the mid-1800s, German Lutherans were arriving in much larger numbers. The Lutheran presence remained strongest in Pennsylvania, but parishes formed in New York, Delaware, Maryland, Virginia, Georgia, as well as the Old Northwest Territory (Ohio, Michigan, Indiana, Illinois, and Wisconsin).

During the 1700s and 1800s, other German-language churches also existed in the same general regions as the German Lutherans. The sometimes-intertwined and often confusing history of these groups can make it more challenging to identify which parish's records might mention your German ancestors. Many Lutheran and Reformed churches united and shared their records. Following the steps outlined in Chapter 2 can help. Call on every clue you have to narrow down the possibilities: Do you already know where they came from and when? Who ministered to them? Who was among their circle of friends? Learn more about these groups in the other chapters on German-language denominations.

Beginning in the mid-1800s, a wave of Scandinavian immigration brought another 2 million or so Lutherans (some in name only) primarily to the Midwest. The Swedes were the largest group, and they first founded churches in Iowa. Norwegians landed in the Upper Midwest, mostly Minnesota and Wisconsin, though they had an Iowa presence as well. Danish Lutherans settled the Midwest and spread to Nebraska, the Dakotas, and eventually California. Finnish immigration, strongest between 1880 and World War I, resulted in the formation of a Finnish Lutheran synod in Michigan.

Many, but not all, ethnically identifiable Lutheran organizations (Germans, Norwegians, Finns, Swedish, Icelanders, Slovaks) eventually merged into the Lutheran Church in America. That body merged with the Association of Evangelical Lutheran Churches and the American Lutheran Church in 1988 to become (by far) the largest Lutheran body in the U.S.: the Evangelical Lutheran Church in America (ELCA), with 4.5 million members. The second-largest organization (with 2.3 million members) is the Lutheran Church—Missouri Synod, founded by German immigrants to the Midwest in 1847.

Smaller Lutheran bodies exist today too. The Wisconsin Evangelical Lutheran Synod, a German group dating from the 1850s in that state, claims nearly 400,000 members. The smaller Church of the Lutheran Brethren of America, founded in 1900 by Norwegian-Americans, has its strongest presence in Minnesota and North Dakota.

A denominational tree of Lutheran bodies in the U.S. is available at http://www.thearda.com/denoms/families/trees/familytree_lutheran.asp.

## ABOUT CONGREGATIONAL RECORDS

Lutheran records are worth looking for! Local records of official pastoral acts (baptisms, confirmations, marriages) tend to be genealogically rich. Many Lutheran parishes also kept membership registers with information about family migrations.

Because of the great diversity and independence of Lutheran churches, there was no set practice for record-keeping or archiving. Each congregation may have done things differently. Records may be in English, Latin, or the immigrants' mother tongue.

*Vital events.* Births were not generally recorded separately in Lutheran records. However, infant baptismal records may include a birth date. Marriages may appear in lists or in narrative (paragraph) format, with the names of the bride and groom, their parents' names, and the dates and location of banns published (sometimes) and the wedding. You may also find birthplaces mentioned (including foreign birthplaces), occupations, residences, and names of witnesses.

Lutherans recorded deaths and, often, funerals and burials. Many churches had their own burial grounds. Sometimes burials were recorded for members who were buried away from their home parish cemetery, or for people from outside the congregation whose burial was overseen by a local minister. You may find a name, maiden name, death date, age, burial date and place, and possibly a former parish, cause of death, information on next of kin and/or survivors (parents, spouses, children), and even the funeral text (usually a scripture verse).

*Membership data.* Registers of congregational membership may list entire families, in groups, with full names, relationships, even birth and death information. Sometimes you'll find multiple generations of a family listed together. Dates of transfer into and out of the church may also be recorded, along with prior or subsequent residence(s). Short biographical sketches of families or individuals may appear here or, if it survived, in a letter of transfer that introduced the new member(s) to the congregation. Many churches kept membership and communion lists that did not always find their way into published versions of the church's records, since they are redundant. (Yet they may have unique information or may help document a family's residence at a specific time.)

Churches also tracked participation in Holy Communion. In colonial times, Communion may have been celebrated twice a year; it became more frequent as time passed. These amount to attendance records and can help you pinpoint more precisely when a family member lived in that parish (or was absent for a time, at least from church participation).

*Baptisms and confirmations.* Infants were often baptized immediately—the day (or the day after) they were born. Where ministers were not nearby, the baptism may have been delayed. You may find the child's birth date, parents' names (including mother's maiden name), number of siblings, and comments on the health or legitimacy of the child. You may also find up to five sponsors named, who were often siblings and other close relatives of the parents. Baptisms of illegitimate children were sometimes recorded separately.

Confirmations of young teenagers (age 13–14) or adults often occurred on Palm Sunday (the Sunday before Easter) or Pentecost (50 days or 7 weeks after Easter). Sometimes these are included with baptismal records and sometimes these are separate. The parents' names and whether they are living are infrequently recorded. Confirmation bestowed full communicant privileges on members: look for their participation in Communion after that.

## HOW TO FIND AND ORDER MEMBERSHIP RECORDS

Begin by contacting existing Lutheran church offices in your ancestor's neighborhood or town, using the steps outlined in Chapter 3. These online congregation locator tools may help:

- ELCA: https://www.elca.org/tools/FindACongregation
- Missouri Synod: http://locator.lcms.org/search.asp
- Wisconsin Evangelical Lutheran Synod: https://wels.net/

When churches merge, the successor church is encouraged to maintain the records. If the records are not with the church and their location is unknown, or if your ancestor's church has closed, try to determine what synod the church belonged to. That piece of information can help you contact the right archive (see Repositories, below). Use the denominational tree mentioned earlier in the chapter to help trace your ancestor's denomination forward or backward in time. Consult Lutheran yearbooks and annuals published during your ancestor's day (see below) for listings of congregations and pastors.

Major denominational archives and online records collections are as follows:

- ELCA: This church has a central archive with an enormous collection of original and microfilmed parish records, mostly from closed and merged parishes. Over 2,000 of these collections (spanning 1875–1940) are searchable on Ancestry (https://search.ancestry.com/search/db.aspx?dbid=60722) and Archives.com (watch a video tutorial on using these at http://www.archives.com/blog/website-updates/using-the-evangelical-lutheran-church-in-america-records.html). This record set is also scheduled to become available on FamilySearch. For additional parish records at the ELCA Archives, search the online catalog at https://www.elca.org/archives/ or contact them through their website. Holdings of ELCA Regional Archives are described at http://download.elca.org/ELCA%20 Resource%20Repository/ELCA_Regional_Archives.pdf.

- Missouri Synod: The Concordia Historical Institute (http://concordiahistoricalinstitute. org/) houses original and/or microfilmed records for many former and active congregations. It also has many transcripts/indexes and congregational histories.

- Records for several individual Lutheran parishes in New York and Pennsylvania are searchable at Ancestry.

- Records for many individual parishes in the Upper Midwest are transcribed online (with original sources given) at http://www.odessa3.org/collections/churches/.

- Locating Lutheranism, a digital archive of Norwegian-American Lutheranism in Minnesota, is online at http://pages.stolaf.edu/locluth/.

- Because no central archive for Lutheran records existed until recent decades, old records may be in private, regional, university, or even state repositories. For example, the Maryland State Archives has a collection of church records (search holdings at http://speccol. msa.maryland.gov/pages/churches/index.aspx).

- If you are researching ancestors in the Wisconsin Evangelical Lutheran Synod, consider contacting its Historical Institute (https://wels.net/about-wels/history/wels-history/).

Many Lutheran church records have been published or at least inventoried in print. Use the strategies in Chapter 3 to locate these. Printed indexes can help you quickly determine whether an ancestor was listed in original records (although, of course, they could miss someone). If original records still exist and are accessible, use the information in the index to find your ancestor's name in the originals. A few print resources for German church records (which include Lutherans) are listed at the end of this chapter.

Finally, be aware that some older German and Scandinavian church records from the U.S. may be written in Fraktur style. Fraktur script can be difficult to read, in part because some letters look deceivingly similar to how other letters are written today. Fortunately, several resources are available to help you interpret Fraktur. A simple Google search of "how to read Fraktur" will return several letter charts and tutorials. See page 82 for more resources on reading Fraktur.

## OTHER RECORDS OF INTEREST

In addition to membership records and official pastoral acts, you may discover details about an ancestor's life in original, microfilmed, or published sources, such as the following:

- Daily journals or logs of ministerial acts performed by ministers or traveling missionaries, which could be kept in addition to registers of acts performed. These may have been kept as a personal possession of the minister or missionary and may or may not have made their way into archival collections; if available, they are sometimes separate from any main collection of the church's records.

- Minutes of the voters' assembly, which in days past was composed of adult male communicants. The voters' assembly handled the administrative functions of a congregation, including discipline and excommunication, the church's property ownership, and even judgments on whether members' divorces would be sanctioned by the church.

- Parish school records, which may include students' names, addresses, and dates enrolled in or attending school; these can help confirm a family's continuing residence there.

- Treasurer's records, which may include lists of donors.

- Congregational histories or regional (synod) histories.

Records about Lutheran ministers may include

- biographical sketches in Lutheran periodicals (see below);
- biographical files and/or collections of personal papers at church or private archives;
- mentions or necrologies of ministers in synod annual yearbooks, synod proceedings, or other records.

*Newspapers.* Many Lutheran synods published their own newspapers. The Library of Congress's Chronicling America newspaper website catalogs just under 100 titles with "Lutheran" in the title. *The German-Language Press of the Americas, 1732–1967* (look for the 2nd edition), by Karl J.R. Arndt and May E. Olson, includes church newspapers. Unfortunately, Lutheran papers did not routinely include obituaries of everyday members. Indexes to a few Lutheran newspaper obituaries have been published. Look for these in WorldCat (see Chapter 3).

*Historical journals.* A few scholarly journals include the history of Lutheranism and are searchable on PERSI (see Chapter 3). Look for a journal that covers a particular synod; for example, *Lutheran Quarterly* for the Evangelical Lutheran Church or *Concordia Historical Institute Quarterly* for the Missouri Synod. Histories of individual congregations and transcriptions of their records are not as common but may exist. Transcriptions of records are more likely to appear in local or regional genealogical journals.

## FURTHER READING

Meynen, Emil, comp. and ed. *Bibliography on the Colonial Germans of North America.* Baltimore: Genealogical Publishing Co., 1982.

Minert, Roger P. *German Immigrants in American Church Records* series. Rockland, Maine: Picton Press, 2005–2012. These include abstracts from records in Indiana, Wisconsin, Nebraska, Iowa, and Illinois.

*Pennsylvania German Church Records of Births, Baptisms, Marriages, Burials, etc. from the Pennsylvania German Society Proceedings and Addresses*, with an introduction by Don Yoder. 3 vols. Baltimore: Genealogical Publishing Co. 1983, reprinted 2009.

Pennsylvania German Society. *Sources and Documents* series (http://www.pgs.org/documents.asp).

Suelflow, August R., Rev., CG, FSAA. "Records of the Lutheran Churches of America," in Church Records of the United States, Part II, World Conference on Records and Genealogical Seminar, Salt Lake City, Utah, 5–8 August, 1969.

Suelflow, August R. "The Lutheran Family in North America," *World Conference on Records: Preserving Our Heritage.* Salt Lake City: The Church of Jesus Christ of Latter-day Saints, 1980.

*Chapter 13*

---

# MENNONITE AND AMISH

---

## QUICK STATS

### FIRST ARRIVED IN THE U.S.:
1683

### DOMINANT REGIONS:
Pennsylvania, Ohio, Indiana, Iowa, Missouri, Kansas, South Dakota, Minnesota

### DOMINANT ETHNIC ORIGIN:
Swiss Mennonites (from Alsace-Lorraine and southwestern Germany, with deeper Swiss roots);
Russian Mennonites (ethnic Germans who lived in the Russian empire); Swiss Amish

## BACKGROUND

The earliest Mennonites in the U.S. colonies arrived in Germantown, Pennsylvania, in 1683. The many-headed Anabaptist movement of which they were a part began 21 January 1525, when Conrad Grebel and his associates committed a heretical act by baptizing one another as adults in Zurich, Switzerland. The term "Mennonite" derives from the name of Menno Simons, one of the early leaders of this Reformation movement in Europe.

Most early Mennonite immigrants came from the Alsace-Lorraine region of France and what is now southwestern Germany, and had deeper Swiss ancestry. For this reason, these immigrants are often referred to as Swiss Mennonites. In the early to mid-1700s, Mennonite families migrated to rural Lancaster County, Pennsylvania, and from there south to Virginia or west toward Ohio, Indiana, Missouri, and Ontario, Canada. Between 1816 and 1875, a large second wave of Mennonites from the area of Basel, Switzerland, came to Ohio and Indiana.

Amish immigrants, members of a conservative group that split from other Swiss Anabaptists in 1693, arrived in Pennsylvania's Berks and Lancaster counties from 1727 through the 1740s. They also gradually moved westward in Pennsylvania and to Ohio and Indiana, where strong communities of Amish still live today.

In the 1870s, Mennonites from the then-Russian empire (now Ukraine) immigrated directly to Kansas, South Dakota, and Minnesota (a few families also went to Nebraska), and also to Manitoba, Canada. Though often called Russian Mennonites, they were ethnic Germans whose ancestors had lived in the Vistula River Valley in what is now Poland, and in the more distant past, in modern-day Belgium and the Netherlands.

Many Mennonite churches have existed in the United States. Historically, Mennonite congregations generally functioned independently, with bishops, elders, and deacons chosen from local members. However, others associated with other Mennonite congregations. In some cases, a Mennonite bishop (a Swiss term) or elder (a Russian term) led more than one congregation. The largest Mennonite church today is the Mennonite Church USA, which united the Russian General Conference with the Swiss Mennonite Church in 2002.

Find a basic denominational tree of Mennonite and Amish groups at http://www.thearda.com/denoms/Families/trees/familytree_mennonite.asp and a more detailed history at the Global Anabaptist Mennonite Encyclopedia Online at https://gameo.org/index.php?title=Mennonite_Church_(MC).

## RECORDS AND HOW TO ACCESS THEM

Historical Mennonite and Amish record-keeping practices varied. Earlier Amish and Swiss Mennonites kept few records because in Europe they could be killed for their beliefs. Later on, congregational membership records were common for many Russian Mennonites and mid-1800s arrivals from modern southwestern Germany.

Some older Mennonite congregational record books have been transferred to a regional Mennonite archive or to the Mennonite Church USA Archives in Elkhart, Indiana (http://mennoniteusa.org/what-we-do/archives/). This repository has a collection of materials relating to the "old" Mennonite Church (MC) and the Mennonite Church USA, as well as some records for Mennonite churches east of the Mississippi River (their records will mainly encompass the Swiss Mennonite stream). Browse its collections from the Mennonite Archival Commons (http://mac.libraryhost.com/).

But congregational record books are not common. Other kinds of records and resources are available for Mennonite and Amish research:

- *Directories* are published at regular intervals. They often contain rich genealogical information on current families and sometimes contain historical information about their communities. Directories can be purchased at local stores and may sometimes be found in local libraries and archives.

- Some *bishops or elders kept personal notes* regarding baptisms, marriages, or communion services; some of these may have ended up in archives.

- Many compiled *cemetery records and obituary collections* exist. Find a directory of links to many Mennonite obituary resources at https://mla.bethelks.edu/holdings/indexes/. The Mennonite Obituary Index (http://www.mhsbc.com/genealogy/mr/mr.htm) has entries from *The Mennonitische Rundschau* (1930–2001), which served a group of Russian Mennonites. Another website, MennObits (http://mcusa-archives.org/mennobits/), covers Amish and Mennonite families with entries dating to 1864. *The Budget* newspaper (http://www.thebudgetnewspaper.com/localnews.html) covers Amish and Mennonite communities; there's a national edition and a local edition. The latter is specific to the Ohio counties of Holmes, western Tuscarawas, southeast Wayne, and northern Coshocton. *The Diary,* based since 1968 in Lancaster County (P.O. Box 88, Kirkwood, PA 17536), has monthly news from North American correspondents, mostly Amish, including births, marriages, and deaths.

- *Published family histories* can prove invaluable too. The Mennonite Historical Library at Goshen (see below) has a large collection of these for the Swiss Mennonites and Amish.

Look also for published Mennonite and Amish family histories in the FamilySearch Catalog online, in WorldCat, and at major research libraries. One example is *Amish and Amish Mennonite Genealogies,* by Hugh F. Gingerich and Rachel W. Kreider (Gordonville, Pa.: Pequea Publishers, 2007; the 1986 edition on HathiTrust has limited search capability), with data on 144 Amish surnames in the United States up to 1850.

- A DNA project exists for those with demonstrated Low German (Russian) Mennonite ancestry. Learn more at http://mennonitedna.com/.

- Periodicals are often filled with scholarly historical articles, newsy stories about local members or congregations, and transcriptions of church records. Titles such as *The Mennonite Research Journal, Mennonite Family History, Pennsylvania Mennonite Heritage* (published by the Lancaster Mennonite Historical Society), *The Mennonite Quarterly Review,* and *The Mennonite Historical Bulletin* are among those indexed in PERSI (see Chapter 3). Another historical resource worth noting is *Mennonita Helvetica,* published in Switzerland.

- *Index to Mennonite Immigrants in Passenger Lists (1872–1904),* by David A. Haury (North Newton, Kan.: Mennonite Library, 1986), may also be of some help.

Networking with others who are researching Mennonite and Amish ancestry can be highly effective, given the relatively small numbers of common ancestors in tightly knit communities that tended to intermarry. Start by visiting these important websites:

- GRanDMA (https://www.grandmaonline.org), short for Genealogical Registry and Database of Mennonite Ancestry, has a database with "information on over a million individuals, most of whose ancestral lines can be traced to Low-German-speaking Mennonite communities in Prussia (now Poland) and South Russia (now Ukraine)."

- SAGA (http://saga-omii.org/), short for Swiss Anabaptist Genealogical Association, has more than 5.8 million tree records covering Swiss Mennonite and Amish ancestors (there is some duplication of individuals across trees).

- Mennonite Genealogical Resources (http://www.mennonitegenealogy.com/) is key for those with Russian Mennonite roots. Connect with others in the active Low German Mennonite Genealogy Forum on various topics, including DNA, getting-started tips, geographic regions, and surnames.

Speaking of important websites, another resource for learning Mennonite history (especially within the context of the Anabaptist movement) is GAMEO, the Global Anabaptist Mennonite Encyclopedia Online (https://gameo.org). As of June 2017, there were more than 16,000 peer-reviewed articles on the site pertaining to history, biography, family history, and other relevant topics.

Several repositories collect Mennonite archival and published materials. It may require some effort to determine which will be most helpful for your research. This list represents the more significant collections:

- Center for Mennonite Brethren Studies at Tabor College (https://tabor.edu/about/center-mennonite-brethren-studies) in Hillsboro, Kansas, preserves the historical legacy of several conferences of the Mennonite Brethren Church, which has Russian Mennonite roots. Among its collections are congregational records, newspapers, and "genealogical and manuscript collections of families and individuals." The site hosts images of a small number of original congregational records and a two-volume printed index to *The Christian Leader,* the first English-language Mennonite Brethren conference periodical.

- The Lancaster Mennonite Historical Society (http://www.lmhs.org/) serves research into Pennsylvania Mennonite and Amish history and genealogy, especially for Lancaster County. Its website includes databases and information about cemetery records, family

Bibles, genealogical papers, obituary indexes, surname files, and other online resources. Its archive is the official repository for the Atlantic Coast and Lancaster Conferences of the Mennonite Church. Search its genealogical card file on Ancestry (https://search.ancestry. com/search/db.aspx?dbid=60592).

- The Menno Simons Historical Library (http://emu.edu/library/historical-library/) archives materials relating to Mennonites and the Shenandoah Valley. It has an extensive genealogical collection and encourages family historians to contact them for assistance. The website hosts digital resources and indexes to offline resources such as obituaries.

- The Mennonite Heritage Center (http://mhep.org/) has archival, library, and artifact collections relating to the eastern Pennsylvania counties of Montgomery, Bucks, Chester, Berks, Lehigh, Northampton, and Philadelphia. The website has a Genealogy Resources page with local history resources, a cemetery database, and lists of periodicals and surnames.

- The Mennonite Historical Library at Goshen College in Indiana (https://www.goshen. edu/mhl) is a starting place for researching Swiss Mennonite and Amish families (both in original archival and library sources). According to its website, the Mennonite Historical Library houses "bibliographies, texts and images on topics related to the Radical Reformation, the Anabaptists, Hutterites, Mennonites, Amish and various related groups." Closely cooperative with this library is the Mennonite Historical Society (https:// mennonitehistoricalsociety.org/), which publishes scholarly research on Mennonite history.

- The Mennonite Library and Archives at Bethel College (https://web2.bethelks.edu/community/ affiliate-organizations/mennonite-library-and-archives/) in Kansas is strongest for the Russian Mennonite groups and includes records for other Mennonite congregations west of the Mississippi River. Browse its archival collections from the Mennonite Archival Commons (http://mac.libraryhost.com/).

- The Mennonite Library & Archives at Fresno Pacific University (http://fresno.libguides. com/mla) in California is the official archives for several Mennonite Brethren churches. Click on the site's Genealogy tab to learn more about its collections of congregational records (including records for "most North American Mennonite Brethren churches that were founded before the 1970s"), family histories, periodicals, and more.

- The Pacific Northwest Mennonite Historical Society Library and Archives (https:// pnmhs.org/archives/) preserves the stories and records of the congregations of the Pacific Northwest Mennonite Conference. According to the site, "Our library of 3,000+ titles includes Mennonite history books, Anabaptist, European, Canadian and American as well as conference and congregational histories. This includes genealogies and family histories. . . . Extensive information is available for congregations in the area, including several extinct congregations. . . . The majority of Mennonites in the area are from Amish Mennonite/Mennonite or General Conference Mennonite background."

- The Illinois Mennonite Heritage Center (https://imhgs.org) in Metamora, Woodford County, Illinois, focuses its collections on "Swiss-German Amish-Mennonite pioneers of 1830–1850 to central and northern Illinois." Its historical and genealogical research library has about 5,000 items.

- Find additional links on the free Cyndi's List Mennonite research page (https://www. cyndislist.com/mennonite/).

In addition, watch for local collections in ancestral communities. For example, the Kidron Community Historical Society Heritage Center in Kidron, Wayne County, Ohio (www.kidron

historicalsociety.org), maintains a genealogy research center with its own database and a collection of local and family histories worth exploring for Mennonite and Amish families from that area.

## FURTHER READING

Beidler, James M. *The Family Tree German Genealogy Guide.* Cincinnati: Family Tree Books, 2014.

Beidler, James M. *Trace Your German Roots Online: A Complete Guide to German Genealogy Websites.* Cincinnati: Family Tree Books, 2014.

Durnbaugh, Donald F. "Pennsylvania's Crazy Quilt of German Religious Groups," *Pennsylvania History* 68:8–30 (Winter 2001).

*Global Anabaptist Mennonite Encyclopedia Online* (https://gameo.org). Includes the full text of the print *Mennonite Encyclopedia*, edited for tense and time context, and continues to add new content from around the world. In June 2017, GAMEO had over 16,000 articles.

Lacopo, Michael D. "Beginning Swiss Mennonite Research," *NGS Magazine* 35 (Jan.–Mar. 2009): 33–38.

Meynen, Emil, comp. and ed. *Bibliography on the Colonial Germans of North America.* Baltimore: Genealogical Publishing Co., 1982.

Minert, Roger P., *German Immigrants in American Church Records* series. Rockland, Me.: Picton Press, 2006–15, 18 vols., and Orting, Wash.: Family Roots Publishing, 2016–18, 7 vols. These include abstracts from records of many different Protestant churches in Indiana, Wisconsin, Nebraska, Iowa, Illinois, Minnesota, South Dakota, North Dakota, Missouri, and Ohio.

*Pennsylvania German Church Records of Births, Baptisms, Marriages, Burials, etc. from the Pennsylvania German Society Proceedings and Addresses*, with an introduction by Don Yoder. 3 vols. Baltimore: Genealogical Publishing Co., 1983; reprinted 2009.

*Chapter 14*

℥

# METHODIST

## QUICK STATS

### CHURCH ORGANIZED IN THE U.S.:
1784

### DOMINANT REGIONS:
Throughout U.S.

### DOMINANT ETHNIC ORIGIN:
English, German, Swedish

### AFFILIATED FAITHS:
Anglican, United Brethren, German Reformed, German Lutheran (Evangelical United Brethren), African Methodist Episcopal, African Methodist Episcopal Zion, Christian (formerly Colored) Methodist Episcopal

## BACKGROUND

English-speaking Methodism began as a movement within the Anglican Church (Church of England) under the leadership of Reverend John Wesley, an Anglican priest. After the American Revolution, Anglicanism lost favor in the United States because of the church's British ties. Methodism gradually separated from its Anglican parent; at the 1784 Christmas conference in Baltimore, leaders organized the Methodist Episcopal Church to fill the vacuum left by the mother church.[1]

Since then, Methodism has experienced many divisions and reunifications on the national level. The earliest of these arose over race relations, with African Americans choosing to meet separately rather than experience discrimination and segregation. In 1794 the Bethel African Methodist Episcopal Church organized in Philadelphia, which eventually led to the founding of the African Methodist Episcopal Church in 1815, now the largest historically African American Methodist denomination in the United States. In 1796 African Americans began meeting separately in New York, which set in motion the formation of the African Methodist Episcopal Zion Church in 1821.

---

1  John H. Wigger, *Taking Heaven by Storm: Methodism and the Rise of Popular Christianity in America* (New York: Oxford University Press, 1998), 23–24.

In 1828 the Methodist Protestant Church separated from the Methodist Episcopal Church. Between 1841 and 1843, another series of splits culminated in the formation of the Wesleyan Methodist Church. The Methodist Episcopal Church, South split from the Methodist Episcopal Church in 1845. After the Civil War, the Colored Methodist Church (now the Christian Methodist Episcopal Church) formed as a separate body from the Methodist Episcopal Church, South.

In 1939 three denominations (Methodist Protestant Church, Methodist Episcopal Church, and Methodist Episcopal Church, South) reunited as the Methodist Church, which itself united with the Evangelical United Brethren Church in 1968 to form the United Methodist Church (UMC). (See the chapter on German Reformed and Sectarian Churches for more on the Evangelical United Brethren Church.) Find a family tree of Methodism at http://www.thearda.com/Denoms/Families/Trees/familytree_methodist.asp.

## ABOUT CONGREGATIONAL RECORDS

The description below applies to practices of the original Methodist Episcopal Church and generally to today's United Methodist Church (the largest Methodist denomination in the United States). There may be variations within and across Methodist traditions.

Methodist ministers were charged as early as 1787 to keep register books with marriages and baptisms, though this wasn't universally practiced. Before the mid-1800s, many Methodists were served by traveling ministers ("circuit riders"), who couldn't carry much with them and may not even have had permanent homes. Early Methodist record-keeping has been described as "chaotic," and many records by itinerant ministers have been lost or are not easy to find. However, many local congregations eventually grew sufficiently to house a minister and keep their own register books on site, and from that point in time, their records may be quite genealogically rich.

Methodist membership records may include baptisms, probationary or preparatory memberships, memberships in full connection, marriages, and funerals.

- Baptism was performed by sprinkling or immersion. Methodist parents were encouraged to have infants baptized as soon as possible. However, Methodism also attracted many adult converts, who were baptized as well.

- Those baptized were considered probationary or preparatory members. For adults, this involved a six-month probationary period (before 1912), during which they were instructed in the Methodist creed and their expected behavior.

- At the end of the probationary period, successful applicants made a profession of faith and were examined, then were recommended to become members in full connection.

Each of these steps is sometimes recorded in membership register books. Additionally, Sunday Schools were popular among Methodists. Many Sunday Schools kept meticulous attendance records, which can be helpful in your search for ancestors.

You'll sometimes find reference to those who discontinued their affiliation with the Methodists. A church member could voluntarily withdraw. The church could also expel members for infractions of contrary belief or conduct.

Administrative policies of the Methodist Church changed over time, including those relating to membership. Fortunately, these policies are well documented in the *Discipline* (*Doctrines and Discipline of the Methodist Episcopal Church*), which is published every four years. The first edition appeared in 1784. Other affiliated churches kept their own versions of this manual. You can find these at annual conference archives, at some major libraries, and in online digital archives such as HathiTrust (htpps://www.hathitrust.org).

## HOW TO ACCESS MEMBERSHIP RECORDS

Use the methods outlined in Chapter 2 to identify your ancestor's local society or church. Use online tools such as the United Methodist Church's Find-a-Church locator (http://www.umc.org/find-a-church/search) to identify the church that today is nearest your ancestor's home. Then consult its website or office to see whether the church is old enough to have served your ancestor.

As a general rule, Methodist records are kept at the local church, if it exists. If a church merged with another congregation, the records were supposed to transfer to the new church. Records of churches that were discontinued or abandoned should have been sent to their annual conference archives (see below). It is also possible they were deposited at private regional archives or historical societies.

United Methodist congregations are organized today into regional bodies known as *annual conferences*. Over time, conference boundaries have shifted; they may contain part or all of a state, or more than one state. Entries for individual congregations in the Find-a-Church locator cited above list the name of the congregation's annual conference and the conference's website.

Each annual conference has an archive; a directory of conference and other archives of Methodism is available at http://www.gcah.org/directories. At conference archives, you will find manuscript or published copies of the annual conference journal, which recorded the doings of the conference. UMC conference archivists may be able to help you locate a church or its records within its boundaries. You can also search a multi-conference archive catalog at http://www.gcah.org/research/search-the-archives, though not all conferences list their closed church records in the UMC catalog.

Many Methodist church records have been microfilmed or published. Look for these as suggested in Chapter 3. Additionally, Ancestry has been working with individual United Methodist annual conferences to digitize and index records in their holdings, which include the records of closed churches. So far, United Methodist collections on Ancestry cover New York, New Jersey, Indiana, parts of New England, Missouri, Illinois, New Mexico, and Texas.

## OTHER RECORDS OF INTEREST

*Records of leadership.* A significant number of Methodists participated in local congregational leadership.

- *Itinerant or traveling ministers* were assigned to travel and preach to multiple churches or preaching places belonging to a circuit, which might span as much as 400 miles in circumference. Follow the progress of ministers' training in conference annual conference journals. After two years of preparation "on trial," successful preachers were admitted in full connection to a conference and ordained as deacons. After two years of service, deacons were eligible for ordination as elders. Conference journals have lists of annual appointments of preachers to circuits, charges, and stations, as well as notations about their deaths, transfers, withdrawals, etc. Obituaries for pastors who died during the year appeared in conference journals. These "memoirs" could be long and flowery, and may also have run in regional Methodist newspapers (see next page). As time went on, ministers' spouses were also memorialized.

  Appointments of itinerant pastors from all over the country also appear in the annual *General Minutes of the Annual Conferences,* available at UMC conference archives, major research libraries, and at the United Methodist General Commission on Archives and History Center at Drew University in Madison, New Jersey (http://www.gcah.org/). The General Commission offers a genealogical research service for obituaries of "full-time, fully ordained clergy" and missionaries (see the website for details). You can also search an online index to their obituaries yourself at http://www.gcah.org/research/search-the-archives.

- *Local preachers* may or may not have been ordained and were not members of the annual conference. Thus, a memoir did not appear in the conference journal following their deaths. But annual conference journals documented their ordination as local deacons and local elders and their recommendations for the itinerancy. You will occasionally find a list of all annual conference local preachers in the conference journal. Their obituaries often appeared in Methodist newspapers.

- *Exhorters, stewards, and class leaders* were local church leaders who participated in church teaching and administration, and provided moral support to members. During the 19th century, local church leaders from each congregation participated with local preachers and traveling (itinerant) ministers in quarterly meetings of a circuit. UMC annual conference archives may have quarterly conference reports for circuits in their manuscript collections. You may find obituaries for exhorters, stewards, class leaders, and local preachers in Methodist newspapers (see below).

Some ministers kept their own records of their travels and ministry: places visited, baptisms or weddings performed, funerals preached, etc. It is rare to find minister's records—they were considered his private papers and may never have been archived with the church. UMC conference archives may have indexes or files on traveling ministers.

*Newspapers.* Regional newspapers were popular among Methodists. In particular, geographic versions of the *Christian Advocate* (*Western Christian Advocate, Pittsburgh Christian Advocate, Central Methodist Advocate,* etc.) are great resources for information on individual churches and preachers. Obituaries of both prominent and everyday church members may appear in these papers. See an example on page 47. Some conference archives have produced indexes to the newspapers. A 2001 "List of Serials Published by Churches Related to the United Methodist Church," compiled by John Baker-Batsel, is available as a free PDF at http://s3.amazonaws.com/gcah.org/UMC_History/Bibliographies/MethList.pdf.

You can find copies of specific issues through Chronicling America's U.S. Newspaper Directory or contact the UMC annual conference archives. The United Methodist Archives and History Center at Drew University (https://www.drew.edu/library/special-collections-archives/umahc/) claims the world's leading collection of Methodist periodicals. They do accept genealogical research requests.

Partial indexes of some papers are available in published or database form: for example, Margaret R. Waters, Dorothy Riker, and Doris Lestner, compilers, *Abstracts of Obituaries in the* Western Christian Advocate *1834–1850* (Indianapolis: Indiana Historical Society, 1988). Search WorldCat, PERSI, and Google for the newspaper's title and the words "index" or "obituaries," or ask at UMC annual conference archives or major research libraries.

## OTHER METHODIST DENOMINATIONS

Some of the same general terminology and practices may apply to other Methodist churches, but the degree to which records are extant and the extent to which they have been collected into central repositories may vary. As noted elsewhere in the book, begin your record search by identifying existing congregations in your ancestor's locale, determining whether they existed at the time of your family's residence, and if so, contacting the church office to see whether they have records.

**African Methodist Episcopal (A.M.E.) Church (https://www.ame-church.com/)**
*Find a congregation:* https://www.ame-church.com/directory/find-a-church/?location=

The Payne Theological Seminary and A.M.E. Archives on the Princeton Theological Seminary's website (http://commons.ptsem.edu/payne) provide digital access to a growing body of historical material on the AME Church and specifically on the clergy who trained at Payne.

**African Methodist Episcopal Zion (A.M.E. Zion) Church (https://amez.org/)**
*Find a congregation:* https://amez.org/church-search/

Livingstone College's Heritage Hall (http://clandy.tripod.com/livingstone/hhall.html) collects historical and archival materials relating to the A.M.E. Zion Church, including minutes, photographs, correspondence, and more. The African Methodist Episcopal Zion Church Collection in the Brooklyn Collection in the Brooklyn Public Library, New York, has a "small but rich collection of papers documenting the financial and administrative affairs of the African Methodist Episcopal (A.M.E.) Zion Church" in the mid-1840s (https://www.bklynlibrary.org/brooklyncollection/finding-aid/african-methodist).

**Christian Methodist Episcopal (C.M.E.) Church (http://www.thecmechurch.org/)**
*Find a congregation:* http://www.thecmechurch.org/churches.html

A collection of materials relating to C.M.E. Church administration (1905–1961) is housed at Paine College (https://www.paine.edu/web/academics/library/finding-aids).

**The Wesleyan Church (https://www.wesleyan.org)**
*Find a congregation:* https://www.wesleyan.org/find-a-church

The Archives of the Wesleyan Church (https://www.wesleyan.org/communication/archives) collects historical materials pertaining to the Wesleyan Church and the Pilgrim Holiness Church, which merged in 1968. It does have information on members of the clergy and missionaries, as well as some local church histories. The archives does not have congregational membership records, which are maintained at the local level. Regional Wesleyan districts do not have archives. If congregational records aren't found locally, contact the archivist through the website for additional suggestions.

## FURTHER READING

Bangs, Nathan. *A History of the Methodist Episcopal Church* (5 vols.) in many editions from 1853.

Campbell, James T. *Songs of Zion: The African Methodist Episcopal Church in the United States and South Africa.* Chapel Hill: University of North Carolina Press, 1988.

Hood, J.W. *One Hundred Years of the African Methodist Zion Episcopal Church, or the Centennial of African Methodism.* New York: AME Zion Book Concern, 1895. Online at The Internet Archive, https://archive.org/details/onehundredyearso00hood/page/ii7.

McEllhenney, John G., et al., eds. *United Methodism in America: A Compact History.* Nashville, Tenn.: Abingdon Press, 1992.

Ness, John Jr. "Church Records of the United States, Part A, Part II, Methodist Records." 4 pp. World Conference on Records: Written, Oral and Traditional History in the USA and Canada as Applied to Research; Genealogical Society of The Church of Jesus Christ of Latter-day Saints. This collection of brief printed talks from 1969 is held at the Genealogy Center, Allen County Public Library, Fort Wayne, Ind.

Schell, Edwin. "Sources for Genealogical Research in Methodist Records." *National Genealogical Society Quarterly* 50:4 (December 1962), 177–82.

## Chapter 15

⚕

# QUAKER
# (Religious Society of Friends)

### QUICK STATS

**FIRST ARRIVED IN THE U.S.:**
1650s–1661

**DOMINANT REGIONS:**
Pennsylvania, North Carolina, New Jersey, New York, Virginia, Maryland, Indiana, Ohio

**DOMINANT ETHNIC ORIGIN:**
English

**AFFILIATED FAITHS:**
Hicksites, Gurneyites, Wilburite, Primitive Friends, Friends United Meeting, Friends General Conference, Evangelical Friends International

## BACKGROUND

A prominent Quaker expert once quipped that anyone who has British colonial U.S. roots dating to 1700 is "almost assured of finding a Quaker forebear."[1] These descendants may discover a treasure trove of meticulous records packed with vital events, intergenerational family relationships, and clues to family migrations.

"Quaker" is the common name for the Religious Society of Friends. Its presence in the U.S. began with a few individuals in the 1650s, but its first organizational appearance was the founding of the New England Yearly Meeting (a regional governing body) in Rhode Island in 1661.

The Quaker movement, which originated in England, was less than ten years old when it arrived in the colonies. English Quakers faced intense persecution because of beliefs and practices that annoyed and threatened the religious and political establishment. Many Quakers fled to the British colonies in America, where they found their positions still unpopular with local Puritan and

---

1 Heiss, Willard, CG, "Quaker Records in America: Records with an Extra Dimension," presented at World Conference on Records and Genealogical Seminar, Salt Lake City, Utah, 5–8 August, 1969, and printed in the *Proceedings: Church Records of the United States*, Part B, Part III, 1.

Anglican churches and some colonists. (Among other things, Quakers opposed bearing arms and paying tithes to an established church.) Their numbers grew among settlers already in America.

Still, the Religious Society of Friends gradually put down roots. Yearly meetings were established in Maryland (1672), Philadelphia (1682), New York and Virginia (both in 1696), and North Carolina (1698). Quakers also migrated into New Jersey, the Carolinas, and Georgia.

By the Revolutionary War, Quakers constituted a significant religious minority in the colonies. But the war itself caused a break in the Society of Friends. In 1781 those who supported the war formed the Free Quakers, who met in Philadelphia until the 1830s.

The Religious Society of Friends continued to grow in the 1800s. Yearly meetings were organized in Ohio in 1813 and Indiana in 1821. In 1827 a major schism resulted in a new branch, the Hicksites, breaking off from the main body, which became known as Orthodox (also referred to as Gurneyite). That group further split in 1845 to form the Wilburite (Conservative) branch. A Primitive Friends group formed in 1860. The plurality of Friends branches by the mid-1800s means that you may need to search the records of more than one local congregation.

Larger affiliations of Friends bodies were formed in the 20th century, some of which eventually reunited earlier factions. Today, Friends organizations in the U.S. include

- Friends United Meeting (the largest Friends body in the U.S., https://www.friendsunited meeting.org);
- Friends General Conference (of the Hicksite tradition, https://www.fgcquaker.org); and
- Evangelical Friends Church (https://www.efcer.org).

The Street Corner Society website has a basic denominational tree for Quakers at http://www.strecorsoc.org/docs/fracture.html, with further descriptions of the various groups and suggested readings.

## ABOUT CONGREGATIONAL RECORDS

The Quaker organizational structure, beginning on the local level, includes preparative meetings, monthly meetings, quarterly meetings, and yearly meetings. A meeting gathers regularly (weekly or more) for worship but the organizational bodies gather monthly (local area), quarterly (regional area), and annually to conduct their business.

Monthly meetings are the basic Quaker administrative unit and may include multiple preparative meetings. The richest Quaker records genealogically are those of monthly meetings. "The monthly meeting undertook to see that justice was done between man and man, that disputes were settled, that the poor were supported, that delinquents, whether as to the Society's own rules or those of the State, were reformed, or if reformation seemed impossible, were 'disowned' by the Society, that applicants for membership were tested and finally, if satisfactorily received, that all children were educated, that certificates of good standing were granted to members changing their abodes, that marriages and burials were simply and properly performed, *and that records were fully and accurately kept*" (emphasis added).[2]

Here's a more detailed description of Quaker records:

- Early records were created in blank books. By the late 1800s, preprinted membership record books were in use.
- Monthly meetings were segregated by gender until after the Civil War, so look for both men's and women's monthly meeting minutes. As they often address similar administra-

2  Isaac Sharpless, *A History of Quaker Government in Pennsylvania*, vol. 1 (Philadelphia, Pa.: Alfred J. Ferris, 1898), 21–22.

tive and social issues, their content may overlap, but one may include details that the other lacks. One may be more legible or accessible. And if one has been lost, perhaps the other is still available.

- The Society of Friends does not practice baptism, so don't bother looking for Quaker baptisms.

- Quakers recorded the births of children born to members in good standing. Entries may mention a place of residence, the father's occupation, and any witnesses of the birth.

- Quaker membership status was either by conviction (a "convinced" member) or by birthright (being born into it). Entries for new members may include birth and marriage information for every member of the family.

- Minutes may mention church disciplinary investigations and consequences for conduct inconsistent with Quaker values. Disowning, or expulsion, was the ultimate penalty.

- Quaker marriage records beginning in the 1700s are quite detailed. In the weeks leading up to the marriage, the bride and groom each applied for permission to marry from their respective women's and men's monthly meetings, where it was recorded in the minutes. Weddings took place during the usual gatherings of monthly meetings, where the couple married themselves (with no minister) in front of all witnesses. The full names of the bride and groom, their parents' names (and whether living), all their places of residence, and the marriage vow itself were written on a marriage certificate, which was signed by the couple and all those present to witness the ceremony. The couple kept the certificate, but its content was copied into the monthly meeting minutes. Early minutes include all who witnessed the wedding, who may or may not have been Quakers.

- Those fully in step with Quaker values did not marry civilly, so civil marriage records won't exist for them. Couples who were both Quakers but married civilly were disowned for marrying "contrary to discipline," but they often sought and received forgiveness and reinstatement. Individuals who married outside the faith ("out of unity") were also disowned.

- Members in good standing who moved out of their monthly meeting area were given certificates of removal or transfer. These included the name of the member's new monthly meeting. Certificates were copied into a book of removals, and then were noted in the new meeting's monthly minutes. Committees may have investigated the financial and legal affairs of members preparing to move, to make sure they left behind no outstanding commitments. Comments on these investigations should appear in the monthly minutes. Additional genealogical details about an entire family may appear when they moved in or out (look in both the men's and women's minutes).

- Members' deaths and burials in Friends cemeteries may have been recorded, perhaps with their parents' names. Funerals were not customary. Early Quakers often did not have tombstones, which were considered ostentatious. Some graves beginning in the 1800s did have stones, but they were simple. Published memorials of deceased members sometimes appeared in print (see Other Records of Interest later in this chapter).

- After the Civil War, Quaker records were not as thorough or consistent. Discipline was not so common. Interfaith marriage was allowed. However, membership transfers generally continued to be recorded faithfully.

- Quaker leadership was unique. Ministers were not formally trained or ordained; they were designated by monthly meetings as those who were particularly faithful and gifted in speaking. Local elders, both men and women, were mature members who provided guidance and oversaw worship meetings. Volunteer administrative responsibilities such as clerking were rotated.

Dates in some Quaker records require some translation. Quakers referred to the days of the week and months of the year numerically (avoiding "pagan" names). The days of the week are easy to calculate: "first day" was Sunday, "second day" was Monday, and so forth.

The months are a little more complicated. Before 1752 the "first month" was March for England and its colonies, which used the Julian calendar system. However, other nations had already transitioned to the Gregorian calendar, as England finally did in 1752. Dates for several years before 1752 often reference both years. "January 1754/55" would indicate a date of January 1754 on the Julian calendar and January 1755 on the Gregorian calendar.

## HOW TO ACCESS MEMBERSHIP RECORDS

Although some local Quaker meetings have held onto their records, most records have been archived and, in turn, published and/or made available or highlighted online. Ancestry's collections for Quakers are extensive; one database alone has more than 6 million names. Ancestry has a Quaker research landing page (http://www.ancestry.com/cs/quakers) with sample images of different kinds of records. Individual record collections on Ancestry include the following:

- "U.S., Quaker Meeting Records, 1681–1935" (http://search.ancestry.com/search/db.aspx?dbid=2189). This extensive collection of partially indexed images of monthly meeting minutes does not index the lists of marriage witnesses. The collection is compiled from original records at the Friends Historical Library at Swarthmore College in Pennsylvania[3]; the North Carolina Yearly Meeting minutes at the Quaker Archives at Guilford College in North Carolina; the Indiana Yearly Meeting Minutes from the Earlham College Friends Collection in Indiana; and the Quaker meeting records collection from Haverford College, Pennsylvania.

- "U.S., Encyclopedia of American Quaker Genealogy, Vols. I–VI, 1607–1943" (http://search.ancestry.com/search/db.aspx?dbid=3753). Almost 357,000 records appear in this collection, sourced from the published compendium of the same name by William Wade Hinshaw (originally published 1936–1950 and reprinted by the Genealogical Publishing Co., 1991–1994). This valuable compilation extracts names, vital events, family relationships, and residences from monthly meeting minutes and, in some cases, adds notes from additional sources such as family Bibles, burial registers, and headstones. If you browse the front matter of each individually imaged volume, you'll find the names of the monthly meetings and other records included in each. Briefly, these include the North Carolina yearly meeting (Vol. 1); New Jersey and Pennsylvania (Vol. 2); New York (Vol. 3); the Ohio yearly meeting (Vol. 4); the Wilmington yearly meeting (covering southwestern Ohio) and the Indiana yearly meeting (Vol. 5); and the Virginia yearly meeting and others (Vol. 6).

- "U.S., Hinshaw Index to Selected Quaker Records, 1680–1940" (https://search.ancestry.com/search/db.aspx?dbid=2705). This database holds nearly 900,000 additional records from the minutes of about 300 monthly meetings not included in Hinshaw's above encyclopedia. Indiana, Iowa, Kansas, Pennsylvania, and New Jersey have the most coverage, but additional monthly meetings from as far west as California and Arizona also appear. Original records are not imaged here (images are of a typed abstract), and they are not geographically comprehensive.

You'll find other Quaker collections online too, though most are indexes and transcriptions rather than digitized images. For example, all records for the New York [state] yearly meeting on file at the Friends Historical Library of Swarthmore College are indexed (http://www.swarthmore.edu/library/friends/hazard/). Conduct online searches for more indexes like these using the strategies in Chapter 3.

To determine what Quaker meetings existed in an ancestor's time and place (and where those records may be now), begin at QuakerMeetings.com (https://quakermeetings.com/Plone/). Every North American monthly meeting that has ever existed is inventoried here. Go to the Search

---

3  Not all Quaker meeting records at Swarthmore are in this Ancestry database. See https://www.swarthmore.edu/friends-historical-library/quaker-meeting-records for a full list of manuscript records at the archive.

page and enter the location. Spell out the state's name in full. You'll see all known meetings for that place, including a note indicating whether the meeting was Hicksite or Orthodox. When you click on a search result, you'll see what records still exist for that meeting and where they are, along with other related online, published, and manuscript records. You'll see how long the meeting has existed, where it's located, and whether it's still active. The names of the different preparatory meetings associated with that monthly meeting are listed under Subordinates. (This site represents an updated version of Thomas C. Hill's 1994 book, *Monthly Meetings in North America: An Index.*)

*Thee & Me: A Beginner's Guide to Early Quaker Records,* by Lisa Parry Arnold, is a recent book with updated links and finding aids for Quaker records in every state. It also includes links to regional Quaker repositories and libraries.

Remember, monthly meeting minutes are the most relevant of records for Quaker genealogy. That said, if you have the privilege of personally reviewing collections of original records at an archive, it's worth looking through the entire collection and its finding aids to see what other documents are available that may shed light on your ancestors.

Many old monthly meeting minutes have been gathered by yearly meetings into centralized archival collections, so you may find yourself looking for the name of a yearly meeting. Also, centralized archives such as those listed toward the end of this chapter tend to collect materials relating to specific branches of Friends, yearly meetings, and/or geographic areas. So here are some tips to help you locate Quaker monthly and yearly meetings (and by extension the branch to which they belonged):

- Though a yearly meeting may be named for a state, its geographic boundaries may not strictly correspond with state boundaries. For example, some monthly meetings in Ohio belonged to the Indiana Yearly Meeting.
- QuakerMeetings.com compiles information about known records and their locations for each monthly meeting.
- Quakermaps.com (http://www.quakermaps.com/) has interactive maps searchable by Friends branch, region, and yearly and monthly meetings.
- Discontinued Quaker meetings are referred to as "laid down."
- Wendy L. Elliott's book *Quaker Research Guide* includes a timeline of yearly meeting changes, especially helpful for those who are looking for yearly meetings organized or reorganized after 1827.
- The Quaker Census of 1828 was created after the 1827 division to document which monthly meetings in the New York yearly meeting became Hicksite and which remained Orthodox. This was published as *Quaker Census of 1828,* edited by Loren V. Fay, AG (Rhinebeck, N.Y.: Kinship, 1989).

Repositories all over the United States collect archival materials on various Friends groups. Here is a partial list, beginning with a description of the focus of each collection:

- Indiana, Western, and Northern Yearly Meetings: Friends Collection and Earlham College Archives, Earlham Libraries (http://library.earlham.edu/ecarchives/).
- North Carolina and Southeast U.S.: Quaker Archives (formerly the Friends Historical Collection, Hege Library, Guilford College (http://library.guilford.edu/archives).
- Hicksite Friends, Philadelphia, Baltimore, and New York Yearly Meetings: Friends Historical Library, McCabe Library, Swarthmore College (https://www.swarthmore.edu/friends-historical-library).
- Philadelphia and Baltimore Yearly Meetings: Quaker & Special Collections, Magill Library, Haverford Libraries (https://library.haverford.edu/places/special-collections/).

- Kansas, Oklahoma, Texas, Missouri, and Colorado: The Quaker Collection, Edmund Stanley Library, Friends University (https://www.friends.edu/academics/library/).
- New England Yearly Meeting: University of Massachusetts Amherst (http://scua.library. umass.edu/umarmot/new-england-yearly-meeting/).
- Ohio Yearly Meeting: Center for Archival Collections, William T. Jerome Library, Bowling Green State University (http://www.bgsu.edu/library/cac.html). Also for the Ohio Yearly Meeting: find its history documented at Quaker Chronicle (http://www.quaker-chronicle. info/).
- National Society, Descendants of Early Quakers (http://www.earlyquakers.org/).

Print inventories to consult cover the following regions:

- Maryland: Jacobsen, Phebe R. *Quaker Records in Maryland* (Annapolis, Md.: Hall of Records Commission, 1966). The FamilySearch Catalog entry for this book links to a digitized version.
- Maryland (north): Peden, Henry C., Jr. *Quaker Records of Northern Maryland: Births, Deaths, Marriages and Abstracts from the Minutes, 1716–1800* (Westminster, Md.: Family Line Publications, 1994).
- Maryland (south): Peden, Henry C., Jr. *Quaker Records of Southern Maryland: Births, Deaths, Marriages and Abstracts from the Minutes, 1658–1800* (Westminster, Md.: Willow Bend Books, 2000).
- Midwest: Heiss, Willard. *Guide to Research in Quaker Records in the Midwest* (Indianapolis: Indiana Quaker Records, 1962).
- New England: Stattler, Richard D. *Guide to the Records of the Religious Society of Friends (Quakers) in New England.* (Providence, R.I.: Rhode Island Historical Society) 1997. An online version of this text is available at New England Yearly Meeting of Friends (http:// neym.org/archives/guide).
- Philadelphia: Eckert, Jack, comp. *Guide to the Records of Philadelphia Yearly Meeting* (Philadelphia, Pa.: Philadelphia Yearly Meeting, 1989). An updated, detailed sequel to this guide is online at Philadelphia Yearly Meeting of the Religious Society of Friends (http://trilogy. brynmawr.edu/speccoll/PYMindex.htm).
- Virginia: White, Miles, Jr. *Early Quaker Records in Virginia* (Baltimore: Genealogical Publishing Co., 1977).

## OTHER RECORDS OF INTEREST

***Memorials and obituaries.*** Quakers often memorialized deceased members in annual memorial books and periodicals. Some were little more than death notices, with a name, age, and death date. Longer memorials have some genealogical information but the emphasis is on a testimonial of that person's religious devotion. Consult the following resources, and be sure to track down images of original records whenever possible, for accuracy and additional information:

- "U.S., Index to Quaker Obituary Notices, 1822–2012" (http://search.ancestry.com/search/ db.aspx?dbid=5349), a card file index to several periodicals. If you don't have access to Ancestry, use the resources below, which cover part of this database:
  - *Quaker Necrology,* two volumes with entries on Conservative or Hicksite Friends from four Quaker periodicals, available in print and on FamilySearch microfilm (see Chapter 3); and
  - American Friend Obituary Index, with memorials for members of the Gurneyite tradition (http://library.earlham.edu/ecarchives/americanfriendobituaryindex).

- "U.S. and UK, Quaker Published Memorials, 1819–1919" (http://search.ancestry.com/ search/db.aspx?dbid=2581), an index to published memorial collections from the Friends Historical Library at Swarthmore College, Guilford College, and Haverford College. This database indexes at least some issues of *The American Annual Monitor, or Obituary of the Members of the Society of Friends in America,* published in the mid-1800s. Digitized (and fully text-searchable) issues for some years are on Internet Archive and HathiTrust Digital Archive (see Chapter 3).

***Scholarly periodicals.*** Historical and genealogical journals include *Bulletin of Friends' Historical Association* (the title was changed to *Quaker History* in 1962); *The Journal of the Friends Historical Society,* and *The Southern Friend: Journal of the North Carolina Friends Historical Society.* Search PERSI for articles in historical and genealogical journals both specific to Friends and to the geographic regions (see Chapter 3).

***Schools.*** In the Quaker tradition, both girls and boys received at least a basic education. Many monthly meetings sponsored a graded school and/or an academy. The monthly meeting records may include minutes of an education committee, though most of these are lost and likely contained little genealogical information. Records of a school itself, including attendance lists and even purchases or loans of textbooks, occasionally still exist. If you find evidence that an ancestor attended or taught at a Quaker college, contact its archive to see what records may exist. Check out the Ancestry database (with half a million records) "U.S., Selected Quaker College Yearbooks and Alumni Directories, 1896–2003" (http://search.ancestry.com/search/db.aspx?dbid=2888).

## FURTHER READING

Arnold, Lisa Parry. *Thee & Me: A Beginner's Guide to Early Quaker Records.* Lisa Parry Arnold, 2014.

Benny, Sally. "Quaker Genealogy," *American Ancestors* (New England Historic Genealogical Society), https:// www.americanancestors.org/education/learning-resources/read/quaker-guide, accessed June 24, 2016. Includes extensive reading list.

Berry, Ellen Thomas, CG, and David Allen Berry, CG. *Our Quaker Ancestors: Finding Them in Quaker Records.* Baltimore: Genealogical Publishing Co., 1987.

Eckert, Jack, comp. *Guide to the Records of Philadelphia Yearly Meeting.* Philadelphia: Philadelphia Yearly Meeting, 1989. An updated, detailed sequel to this guide is online at Philadelphia Yearly Meeting of the Religious Society of Friends, http://web.tricolib.brynmawr.edu/speccoll/PYMindex.htm.

Elliott, Wendy L., CG. *Quaker Research Guide.* Bountiful, Utah: American Genealogical Lending Library, 1987.

Heiss, Willard C., CG. "American Quaker Records and Family History," presented at the World Conference on Records, "Preserving Our Heritage," August 12–15, 1980, Series 358.

Heiss, Willard C., CG, and Thomas D. Hamm. *Quaker Genealogies: A Selected List of Books.* Boston: New England Historic Genealogical Society, 1985.

Heiss, Willard, C., CG. "Quaker Records in America: Records with an Extra Dimension," presented at World Conference on Records Genealogical Seminar, Salt Lake City, Utah, 5–8 August, 1969, and printed in the Proceedings: Church Records of the United States, Part B, Part III, pp. 1-11.

Hinshaw, William Wade. *Encyclopedia of American Quaker Genealogy,* 6 vols. 1936–1950. Reprint, Baltimore: Genealogical Publishing Co., 1991–1994. *See* the Ancestry database "U.S., Encyclopedia of American Quaker Genealogy, Vols. I–VI, 1607–1943" mentioned above.

Russell, Elbert. *The History of Quakerism.* New York: Macmillan, 1943. Or find it on the HathiTrust Digital Library, https://www.hathitrust.org.

"Research Guide to Finding Your Quaker Ancestors." Ancestry, https://www.ancestrycdn.com/mars/landing/ quaker/quaker-guide.pdf.

Stattler, Richard D. *Guide to the Records of the Religious Society of Friends (Quakers) in New England*. Providence, R.I.: Rhode Island Historical Society, 1997. An online version of this text is available at New England Yearly Meeting of Friends, https://neym.org/archives/guide.

Thomas, Allen C., and Richard H. Thomas. *A History of the Society of Friends in America*. Philadelphia: John C. Winston Co., 1895. Or find it at Internet Archive, https://archive.org/.

White, Miles, Jr. *Early Quaker Records in Virginia*. Baltimore: Genealogical Publishing Co., 1977.

# Chapter 16

❦

---

# PRESBYTERIAN

---

## QUICK STATS

### FIRST ARRIVED IN THE U.S.:
About 1684

### DOMINANT REGIONS:
Mid-Atlantic, Pennsylvania, Virginia, Appalachians, and Midwest

### DOMINANT ETHNIC ORIGIN:
Scottish, Scots-Irish, English, Northern Irish (often Scottish origin)

### AFFILIATED FAITHS:
Congregationalist

## BACKGROUND

The term "Presbyterian" refers to a type of government by member-elected elders (*presbuteros* in Latin) rather than appointed bishops, etc. Such a philosophy resonated well with colonists and early Americans and helps explain how Presbyterianism grew so quickly.

Presbyterianism first spread from the mid-Atlantic region: Maryland, New York, New Jersey, Pennsylvania, and Virginia. The first American presbytery was organized in Philadelphia in 1706. Membership grew steadily until the Revolution, along with the gradual arrival of about 200,000 overwhelmingly Presbyterian Scots-Irish (also called Scotch-Irish and Ulster Scots), whose prime destination was Pennsylvania.

Local governing bodies of congregations were known as *sessions*. The first presbytery, or group of congregations, was organized in Philadelphia in 1706 and the first synod (group of presbyteries) was organized ten years later. The first General Assembly, composed of four synods, was organized in 1789, under the banner of the Presbyterian Church in the United States of America. Other Presbyterian sects also formed throughout the 1700s and 1800s.

After the Revolutionary War, Presbyterian churches dotted the frontier. They welcomed Congregationalists arriving from New England who didn't have local churches. In 1801 the two churches formally united for a few decades, so you may find the records of one among the records of the other.

During the 1800s and 1900s, many strands of Presbyterianism united and divided. Here's a summary from the Presbyterian Historical Society:

> Currently the largest group is the Presbyterian Church (USA), which has its national offices in Louisville, KY. It was formed in 1983 as a result of reunion between the Presbyterian Church in the U.S. (PCUS), the "southern stream," and the United Presbyterian Church in the U.S.A. (UPCUSA), the "northern stream." The UPCUSA was formed by the merger (1958) of the Presbyterian Church in the United States of America, descending from the Philadelphia presbytery of 1706, and the United Presbyterian Church of North America, which had been constituted (1858) by a union of two older churches [the Associate Reformed Synod and the Associate Presbyterian Synod]. Other Presbyterian churches in North America include: the Presbyterian Church in America, the Orthodox Presbyterian Church, the Evangelical Presbyterian Church, the Cumberland Presbyterian Church, the Cumberland Presbyterian Church in America, the Associate Reformed Presbyterian Church, and the Presbyterian Church of Canada.[1]

Find a Presbyterian denominational tree at http://www.thearda.com/denoms/families/trees/familytree_presbyterian.asp. Or check out a differently formatted tree in Chapter 3.

## ABOUT CONGREGATIONAL RECORDS

Presbyterian records can be quite valuable genealogically, though there may be restrictions on records less than 50 years old. Here's what you may find in older records:

*Vital events.* Vital events of Presbyterian members are often scattered through membership registers and session minutes (described below). Separate lists of marriages may exist with the couples' names, the date, and sometimes other information such as residents, witnesses' names, and parents' names and residences. Deaths may be mentioned in membership or baptismal lists, and sometimes there are burial lists or cemetery plot sales.

*Membership lists.* These generally include names and sometimes evidence of spousal relationships. There may be details about when members moved in and out—and sometimes where they went or from whence they came. You may learn whether they were received by examination or profession (meaning they were new to the faith and were likely current residents) or by certificate or letter (meaning they came with a letter of recommendation from another Presbyterian church, thus probably recent arrivals).

*Baptisms.* Baptismal records include "infants" (meaning children, not necessarily babies) and adults. Baptism didn't grant full membership in the church. Children's baptismal records often did not include their ages or birth dates but did note parents' names. Often several children from one family were baptized on the same day.

*Communion rolls or registers.* These are lists of those who participated in Communion and were full members of the church. These do not routinely contain vital events or family relationships, but occasionally you may find a mention or evidence that an active member left town or otherwise stopped participating in Communion.

*Session minutes.* Session minutes document ongoing administrative and ministerial activities of the local sessions. These may mention a member's death or marriage, along with members' migrations (in or out). Members were often mentioned along with their roles at the church, like committee membership, chorister, or "tithing man." Separation from the church—suspension or excommunication, often for non-attendance or "bad moral character"—may also be documented here.

---

1 "History of the Church," *Presbyterian Historical Society/The National Archives of the PC(USA)*, https://www.history.pcusa.org/history-online/presbyterian-history/history-church.

## HOW TO ACCESS MEMBERSHIP RECORDS

Original membership records are typically kept by local congregations. If you know the name of the church, contact its office using the tips in Chapter 3. Or try one of the following databases:

- Current congregations of the Presbyterian Church (USA), http://www.pcusa.org/search/congregations/

- Current and past congregations of Cumberland Presbyterian Churches, http://www.cumberland.org/hfcpc/churches/

- Current (and oldest 50) congregations of the Presbyterian Church in America, http://www.pcahistory.org/churchindex.html

If you have a family record containing the name of a Presbyterian minister, one of the archives or libraries listed below may be able to help you identify the church with which he was affiliated. Since congregations may have changed their names through moving or merger, you may also contact the stated clerk of the presbytery (local regional body) for assistance in locating church records.

If you don't know the name of the church or minister, use strategies previously described to locate the local Presbyterian congregation of your ancestor's day. "Hall's Index of American Presbyterian Congregations" is an index to the names and locations of both current and dissolved congregations. Search it for free at https://www.history.pcusa.org (under Collections > Research Tools). Another helpful index on that same site is the "Congregation and Other Organization Vertical File Index," an index of files documenting individual Presbyterian churches, presbyteries, and more since 1850 (under Collections > Online Catalogs). This database does include records from other Presbyterian denominations.

If you don't find church records with the congregation, look first to the Presbyterian Historical Society (PHS, https://www.history.pcusa.org/) in Pennsylvania. Formed in 1852, today the society has a large number of congregational records. Records for Illinois, Maryland, New Jersey, New York, North Carolina, and Pennsylvania are listed on the Church Record Surveys page of its website (http://www.history.pcusa.org/collections/research-tools/church-record-surveys). Contact reference staff or search its online catalog for the hundreds of records it holds for other states.

Presbyterian seminaries also have archived some congregational records. Of particular note is the collection at the Columbia Theological Seminary (https://www.ctsnet.edu/library/collections-and-archives/congregational-records/), which includes a large collection of congregational records from Southern states that was transferred from the Presbyterian Historical Society facility in Montreat, North Carolina, in 2007. These records do include some from other Presbyterian denominations. Several Presbyterian seminaries have published biographical directories of their alumni, which may be found through searching the web.

The Presbyterian Heritage Center (http://www.phcmontreat.org/) collects materials relating to the history of Presbyterianism. They maintain an archive but they do not collect original congregational records, which are sent to the Presbyterian Historical Society or a Presbyterian seminary.

Remember, the Presbyterian Church (USA) represents the *largest* Presbyterian faith group in the United States but not the *only* one. You may find yourself browsing the websites or contacting central offices or archives such as

- Cumberland Presbyterian Church Historical Library and Archives (https://www.cumberland.org/hfcpc/hla.htm);

- PCA Historical Center: Archives and Manuscript Repository for the Continuing Presbyterian Church (http://www.pcahistory.org/); and

- Reformed Presbyterian History Archives: History Committee of the Synod of the Reformed Presbyterian Church of North America (http://rparchives.org/), a website that includes digitized church publications and lists of ministers.

Even if other denominational archives don't house original congregational records, they may be able to help you determine the name of the church, which may then help you locate the records in other repositories.

Many old Presbyterian records are searchable (through NUCMC or ArchiveGrid); microfilmed or published in books (at WorldCat or the FamilySearch Catalog); or published in journals (searchable through PERSI). Read more about all these resources in Chapter 3.

## OTHER RECORDS OF INTEREST

In addition to the membership records already described, you may find mentions of ancestors in other original records of the church. Once you locate membership records, ask the records custodian whether pew rental records, donation or subscription lists, cemetery plot sales, or other records exist. Such a request may be fruitful in your research and may also set you apart in their mind from genealogists who are only chasing names.

Ask congregational offices or archives whether they have congregational histories, newsletters, anniversary or commemorative programs, or other printed materials. The Austin Seminary Archives (https://www.austinseminary.edu/page.cfm?p=1688) has a collection of church histories that is particularly strong for Texas, Oklahoma, Arkansas, and Louisiana.

If you are researching a Presbyterian minister, home missionary, or active lay person, look for them in the following:

- Rolls of church officers (elders, trustees, treasurers, or clerks of the congregation or session) among the congregational membership records. You may find their beginning and end dates of service.

- The Biographical Vertical Files index on the PHS website. Use the information you find there to request copies of the files.

- Sketches of ministers (1888–1930) and a list of Covenant ministers (1930–1963) at the Reformed Presbyterian History Archives website (http://rparchives.org/).

- *The Encyclopedia of the Presbyterian Church in the United States of America: Including the Northern and Southern Assemblies* (1884). It includes short biographies of clergy and prominent laymen. Look for this in research libraries or consult the digitized version at Internet Archive (https://archive.org/details/encyclopaediaofp00nevi).

- *Ministerial Directory of the Presbyterian Church, U.S., 1861–1983* (1986) and four previous editions, for sketches of PCUS ministers. The 1941 and 1951 editions are fully searchable at HathiTrust (https//www.hathitrust.org/), and the 1898 edition is online at Internet Archive.

- Glasgow, William M. *Cyclopedic Manual of the United Presbyterian Church of North America.* Pittsburgh: United Presbyterian Board of Publication, 1903. Available at Internet Archive.

- Kelsey, Hugh Alexander. *The United Presbyterian Directory: A Half-Century Survey, 1903–1958.* Pittsburgh, Pa.: Pickwick Press, 1958.

- Glasgow, William M. *History of the Reformed Presbyterian Church in America. . . .* Baltimore: Hill & Harvey, 1888.

In the 1800s, Presbyterians were known for their evangelical, educational, and reform societies. They sent missionaries abroad and to African American and Native American communities.

These auxiliaries created records. Foreign missionaries appear in the Index to Foreign Missionary Personnel Files on the PHS website.

Some Presbyterian newspapers contained genealogical information. For example, a German newspaper in Dubuque, Iowa, *Der Presbyterianer,* had marriages and obituaries. Over 150 Presbyterian newspapers are indexed on Chronicling America (https://chroniclingamerica.loc.gov/). Search its US Newspaper Directory, 1690–Present by city or by the name "Presbyterian" to find papers that may have covered an ancestor's area, along with information about where to find copies of those papers. The Special Collections department at the Burke Library at Union Theological Seminary (https://library.columbia.edu/locations/burke/using-special-collections.html) houses many 19th-century newspapers published in the South; the Presbyterian Historical Society does so for the North. (It could be a long trek if they are not digitized; check for this status as the situation changes frequently.)

When researching the history of a congregation (especially an older one) or a minister, consider searching the *Journal of Presbyterian History.* In print for over 100 years, several issues are digitized on HathiTrust. The easiest way to search it is through PERSI (see Chapter 3). Use the filter for Periodicals to select that title and then run a search with your location, names, or keywords.

## FURTHER READING

Bankhurst, Benjamin. *Ulster Presbyterians and the Scots Irish Diaspora, 1750–1764.* Part of the series *Christianities in the Trans-Atlantic World, 1500–1800.* New York: Palgrave Macmillan, 2013.

Hoefling, Larry. *Chasing the Frontier: Scots-Irish in Early America.* New York: iUniverse, 2005.

Longfield, Brad J. *Presbyterians and American Culture: A History.* Louisville: Westminster John Knox Press, 2013.

Miller, William B. "Presbyterians," in Church Records of the United States, Part III, World Conference on Records and Genealogical Seminar. Salt Lake City, Utah, 5–8 August, 1969.

# Chapter 17

§

# ROMAN CATHOLIC

## QUICK STATS

### FIRST ARRIVED IN THE U.S.:
1540

### DOMINANT REGIONS:
Urban and most locales outside the Deep South

### DOMINANT ETHNIC ORIGIN:
Spanish, French, German, Irish, Italian, Polish, Slovakian, Slovenian

## BACKGROUND

The Roman Catholic Church had a presence in the middle part of North America centuries before the United States existed as a nation. Spanish Catholics entered what is now New Mexico in 1540 and Florida in 1595. By about 1634, the first English Catholic settlers arrived in Maryland.[1] Catholicism grew fortyfold from 1800 (a single diocese of 50,000 members) into a major denomination by 1860 (over 2 million communicants in 44 dioceses).[2]

The church grew primarily by natural increase and immigration (German, Irish, and, later, Italian and eastern European), rather than by evangelism. Its quasi-monarchical structure was not always a comfortable fit with democracy-minded worshipers at other altars in the United States. During the 1800s, Catholics at all levels had to deal with both diversity within their own flock and hostilities from nativist (and often racist) Protestants.

## ABOUT CONGREGATIONAL RECORDS

Catholic sacramental records are some of the best-preserved church records in the United States and among the richest in genealogical information. (In many locales, they predate governmental vital records.) Baptismal, marriage, death, and other records may exist. Until preprinted register books became available in the late 1800s, sacramental records were often handwritten in blank books. The records may be in Latin or in the language of the priest or parish; consult foreign-lan-

---

1   Catherine L. Albanese, *America: Religions and Religion* (Belmont, Calif.: Wadsworth Publishing Co., 1981), 61, 63.
2   Robert T. Handy, *A History of the Churches in the United States and Canada* (New York: Oxford University Press, 1976), 214.

guage genealogical word lists online, such as those in the FamilySearch wiki, for help translating key words and phrases. But words can change meaning in different contexts; consider seeking professional help rather than guessing.

*Baptisms.* Catholics practice infant baptism. Baptismal records should contain the name, parents' names, date of baptism, and the name of the officiating priest. Often they contain the date of birth of the baptized and the mother's maiden name. Parents' birthplaces may be noted, especially for immigrant families in ethnic parishes. In areas of French or Spanish influence, the grandparents' names sometimes appear. Information about certain later sacramental events (such as confirmation, marriage, or holy orders/vows) is supposed to be sent by later parish priests back to the parish of baptism, but this doesn't always happen. See a sample Catholic baptismal record on page 5.

"Emergency baptisms" are performed when a newborn is in mortal danger. A midwife or anyone else may perform this baptism at a home, hospital, or wherever. If the infant survives, a follow-up ceremony is held at the church. The baptism itself is not repeated. The infant's name is entered in the baptismal register. There should be an annotation that an emergency baptism took place, as well as when and by whom.

*Marriages.* Marriage records usually contain the names of the bride and groom, wedding date, names of witnesses, and the name of the priest who married them. Sometimes an overseas town of origin is noted. In some times and places, marriage banns were read three times during Mass (see Chapter 1). This requirement could be waived in special circumstances (i.e., the groom suddenly being called into military service). Waiving required a dispensation, or special permission, from the church.

Very few written registers of banns exist in the U.S. You may find mention of banns or dispensation of them in original marriage records. Separate record books may be kept for dispensations of all kinds. Material from these books may or may not be considered confidential, depending on the time period and the nature of the information recorded. Dispensations may be mentioned in prenuptial files (see below).

Look first for marriage records in the bride's parish, which traditionally hosted the wedding. If you can't find a church marriage record, look for the baptismal record.

## HOW TO ACCESS MEMBERSHIP RECORDS

Extant Catholic sacramental records are generally maintained at parishes or, if the parish has closed, at a diocesan or archdiocesan archive. They are private and traditionally considered confidential. If you request records, you may or may not be granted access. Even if you are granted access, the records supplied may be transcriptions on typed certificates; some information may be withheld.

Canon law governs the creation and maintenance of Catholic records. You will usually not be allowed to view potentially confidential information created in recent decades. However, actual practice varies greatly among dioceses. The Archdiocese of Seattle spells out its policy on sacramental records more clearly than most (http://www.seattlearchdiocese.org/Archives/records/sacguidelines.aspx). A growing number of indexed and/or digitized Catholic sacramental records are available online, including the following:

- The Boston Archdiocese and the New England Historic Genealogical Society are currently creating an online searchable database of millions of sacramental records from over 100 parishes across greater Boston from 1789 to 1900 (https://catholicrecords.americanancestors.org/).

- Findmypast hosts the Catholic Heritage Archive (https://www.findmypast.com/catholic records), home to a growing number of diocesan and archdiocesan collections, currently from Philadelphia, New York City, Baltimore, Cincinnati, and Chicago. Additional ones are planned from Wilmington and Toledo (Ohio).

- FamilySearch has digitized a growing number of previously microfilmed Catholic parish records. Search the FamilySearch Catalog (https://www.familysearch.org/search/catalog/search) by locale, and then by record type (church records). Scroll down in individual catalog entries to see whether an item is available in digitized format. Items in the FamilySearch Catalog that aren't online are generally available on microfilm at the Family History Library in Salt Lake City.

- Local initiatives will differ. For example, in Indiana the Diocese of Fort Wayne and South Bend has microfilmed sacramental records from 1830 to 1940; researchers must query the archivist, who will search the records on their behalf (http://www.diocesefwsb.org/Diocesan-Archives). The Diocese of Gary offers no link to archives or an archivist, but does provide a list of where closed parishes' sacramental records are now located (http://www.dcgary.org/sacramental-records-closed-parishes.htm).

Some dioceses or parishes may deliberately choose not to make records available online, for reasons of confidentiality or privacy.

Bear in mind that parish offices are busy with pastoral care for *living* parishioners. They are not professional archivists or historians, and genealogy requests are not a high priority for them. Your request may take some time to answer. You will likely be asked to fund administrative staff time for fulfilling your requests. The records may not be indexed, and parishes will not generally do extensive research. You'll need to provide as much specific information as you can about the people and dates of interest.

Parish records may be incomplete or nonexistent for all the usual reasons. Diocesan archives may not be complete either; usually they have only what they are given by the parishes. These archives are not public research libraries with open stacks. Access will likely be by appointment only, and limited in length by their staffing and scheduling needs.

Use the methods outlined in Chapter 2 to identify your ancestor's parish (congregation). *The Official Catholic Directory*, an annual first published in 1817, can be very helpful. If you locate the name of a priest who performed a wedding or other sacrament, you can look up the priest's assigned parish in that same year's directory. (Chapter 2 demonstrates this process.) Besides listing all the priests, *The Official Catholic Directory* has a necrology of priests who died that year. It also lists the different religious orders for men and women. Old directories can help identify diocesan boundaries and the parish an ancestor most likely attended.

Catholic parishes had geographic boundaries until the early 1960s, when the historic Vatican II conference resulted in many changes in the Church. Beginning in the late 1800s, however, the Vatican made an exception, allowing U.S. Catholics to choose parishes based on their native language. These parishes served parishioners in their native tongues, observed native religious traditions and saints, and created enclaves of a common cultural identity. In addition to *The Official Catholic Directory*, look for ethnic and national parishes in city directories and maps from your relatives' era.

If the parish still exists, search for it online using parish name, city, and state. Alternatives include Parishesonline (https://www.parishesonline.com/) or a current *Catholic Directory*.

Parishes that closed (often mentioned in Parishesonline) likely sent their records to the diocesan offices, a neighboring parish, or the parish resulting from a merger. Contact the diocesan archive to find out where those records went. (Some areas' regional government is an archdiocese, generally larger and more historically important or powerful than a diocese.) Virginia Humling's *U.S. Catholic Sources: A Diocesan Research Guide* is slightly dated (1995) but can help you determine the geographic area covered by various dioceses.

Once you have reached the point of asking the right person in the right place for the right record, consider four additional options:

1.  If you are already aware of private family information that may appear in the records you're requesting (such as births out of wedlock or adoptions), mention this when you request a record. The staff may more freely share data with you once they learn you are already aware of a situation.

2.  If the staff member is transcribing information from the original record onto a certificate for you, politely request that they include *all* non-confidential information contained in the original (such as parents' birthplaces or parish of baptism), even if it has to be written in the margins of the transcribed certificate. This information may help the transcriber to understand that you are seeking information, not an elegant wall hanging.

3.  If you have specific research questions—like a woman's maiden name or the parents' birthplaces—convey that in your research request. Archivists may be more likely to include that information if they see it. They may even have access to other records that could answer the question.

4.  When requesting records from before 1930, politely ask whether they'd be willing to send a photocopy or digital image of just your ancestor's record (cropped to exclude surrounding records). You might be pleasantly surprised!

## OTHER RECORDS OF INTEREST

***Other sacramental records.*** Registers noting First Communion and Confirmation generally do not contain unique genealogical information, except to confirm the child's residence and participation in church life. Sponsors' names may be listed. These records are not indexed and may be difficult to locate unless you know the approximate date of the event. Children often received First Communion at age 8 and were confirmed around the age of 13.

Those interested in a relative's spiritual life may find these valuable. Also, the parish (or diocese for closed parishes) often has group photos of First Communion or Confirmation classes. It's worth asking about.

***Annuals and histories.*** Some parishes produced annual or occasional yearbooks or membership directories. Commemorative histories were also written for important anniversaries (25, 50, 100 years) celebrated by parishes and dioceses. Look for these on the parish and/or diocesan level, in good genealogical libraries, and at universities with Catholic collections.

Some historical information may be available online. For example, the Diocese of Dallas website (https://www.cathdal.org/teacherresources) contains a history of the diocese, a timeline of significant events, and *They Came to Serve: A Chronology of Women Religious in the Catholic Diocese of Dallas 1874–2014*, which includes history, photos, and a timeline.

The University of Notre Dame's Archives has a collection of parish histories representing more than 2,000 parishes (http://www.archives.nd.edu/about/news/index.php/2010/catholic-parish-history-collection). Separately held in the Theodore M. Hesburgh Library are histories and newspaper accounts for 1,300 parishes. While these histories provide a broader context, they rarely include information about individual parishioners.

***Burial records.*** Roman Catholic cemeteries keep administrative records of burials. These generally include the name of the deceased, date of death, and burial date and place. You may find additional notes as well, such as the age at death or cause of death. Some burial records may remark whether the deceased received the sacrament of the anointing of the sick, formerly known as extreme unction, before death. (Parishes do not otherwise keep regular records of the sacrament of the anointing of the sick.) Such comments are more likely found in older record books, which were less regulated. Here's a series of two entries from a 1906 burial register:[3]

> Doto: On April 4, 1906, Angelo Doto died, and was buried April 5 in our cemetery, having aged 23 years.

> Pille: On April 17, 1906, Henry Pille died, his age 67 years, having been provided all of his mortal sacraments. He was buried on April 19th, in the Ashland Protestant Cemetery.

Catholic cemetery records are often maintained at a single cemetery association office for the entire diocese. Some of these organizations have websites with information on what records are available, what's in them, and how to request them; some even have searchable burial databases. Plot purchase records, burial lists of those in family plots (including stillborn infants whose lives may be otherwise undocumented), cemetery plot maps, and other resources may be available. The St. Louis Archdiocese has a searchable list of burials in the seventeen area cemeteries it operates (https://cemeteries.archstl.org/Home)—especially valuable, as its search function includes everyone buried in a given plot.

***Censuses.*** Censuses of parishioners have been taken occasionally in some parishes and/or dioceses, especially during times of transition or reorganization. These may include residence address, occupation, and/or notes about members' participation in church life. These are not comprehensive lists of every household member, like recent U.S. federal censuses. For instance, the Pittsburgh Diocese's 1877–1970 censuses "contain only the numeric count of individuals registered with a particular parish," according to WorldCat. Diocesan archivists may know of these. Creative searching for published or microfilmed censuses at WorldCat, FamilySearch, or other record providers (see Chapter 3) may also help.

***Church minutes.*** The minutes or administrative records of parish auxiliary organizations and councils for recent decades (post-Vatican II) may be found in parish offices. These are most helpful for researching the religious participation of relatives known to be active in the church community.

***Profession of faith.*** Someone previously baptized in another Christian faith may join the Catholic Church with a profession of faith. If this could have been the case with your relative, request a search of these records, if they were kept separately.

***Records of priests and nuns.*** The sacrament of holy orders and the taking of vows represent the transition to full-time religious life as a priest or nun. These are celebrated with a sacrament in the man or woman's current parish, which should send a record of it back to the parish of baptism. After orders are taken, the archive of the motherhouse of the religious order that person joined is the place to check for information. The motherhouse may be located anywhere and send its members anywhere. Orders generally keep excellent biographical and genealogical information on those who join their ranks. Search online for the name of the order. If you have difficulty locating the motherhouse or its archive, contact a diocesan or archdiocesan archivist in a place where that order had a presence. See the *Catholic Directory* for a given year for information on religious orders for men and women.

***School records.*** Catholic elementary and secondary schools have played a major role in Catholic life beginning in the 19th century, especially among immigrant families. School records, if pre-

---

3 Death records, St. Peter's Catholic Church, Loudonville, Ashland County, Ohio; photocopies, Ohio Genealogical Society Library, Bellville, MSS 197, folder 4, n. p.

served, would be with the parish, diocese, or religious order that ran the school. If the school or its organization is defunct, check the diocesan education office in that area. School transcripts are generally considered confidential. Photographs, enrollment lists, school histories, yearbooks, news clippings, and other school memorabilia may be available. For Catholic colleges and universities, contact the school archives. Similar limitations may apply.

*Tribunal records.* The diocesan tribunal office is a church court of sorts that governs annulments and other situations that require judgment. In the United States, tribunals were authorized in 1883 but were not always established immediately.

Tribunal offices may have prenuptial files created during a couple's preparation to marry. These should contain copies of baptismal certificates, marriage certificates, any documents relating to an annulment, and more. These are confidential files, but may be something a staff member could access in the process of researching your kin. Marriage dispensation documentation in prenuptial files may yield a treasure trove of genealogical information. See the citation for an interesting article on marriage dispensations by Dan McDonald in the Further Reading section below.

*Newspapers.* The Catholic News Archive (https://thecatholicnewsarchive.org) has digitized searchable material from newspapers across the country, with issues dating back to 1831.

## FURTHER READING

Doyle, John J. *Genealogical Use of Catholic Records in North America.* Indianapolis: Indiana Historical Society, 1992.

Findlen, George. "The 1917 Code of Canon Law: A Resource for Understanding Catholic Church Registers." *National Genealogical Society Quarterly* 93 (Sep. 2005): 126–47. Some knowledge of canon law can illuminate difficult cases.

Galles, Duane L.C.M. "Roman Catholic Church Records and the Genealogist." *National Genealogical Society Quarterly* 74 (Dec. 1986): 271–78. A thorough introduction.

Hughes, Christine Human. *Guide to St. Louis Catholic Archdiocesan Parish Records.* St. Louis: Friends of St. Louis County Library, 2001. This exemplary guide covers ten counties and the city of St. Louis.

McDonald, Dan. "Some Notes on Marriage Dispensations in Roman Catholic Marriage Records," *The Brick Walls,* http://www.brikwall.com/marrdispensations.html.

# INDEX

Spanish colonists, 16
tribunal records, 134
cemeteries, churchyard, 52–53
Center for Mennonite Brethren
Studies, Tabor College, 105
Charis Fellowship, 83
charitable organizations, 51
CHL. *See* Latter-day Saint, Church
History Library
*Christian Advocate*, 112
*Christian Intelligencer*, 47, 79
*Christian Leader*, 105
Christian Methodist Episcopal
Church, 110, 113
Christian Reformed Church in
America, 77
Chronicling America. *See* Library
of Congress
church affiliation
and ethnicity, 3–4
mentioned in family
documents, 14
ways to identify, 13–21
*Church Herald*, 79
*Churchman*, 61
Church of England, 57–58
marriage banns, 6
ministers, names of, 61
missionaries, colonial-era, 61
*See also* Anglican; Episcopal;
Methodist
church offices, contacting, 23–25
Church of Jesus-Christ of Latter-day
Saints, The. *See* Latter-day Saint
Church of the Brethren. *See*
Brethren
Church of the Lutheran Brethren
of America, 98
Church of the United Brethren in
Christ, USA, 89
church records
administrative, 48
auxiliary, 51
by-laws, 48
creeds, 48
digital, 39, 26–27
founding documents, 49
guidelines for using, 42–44
handwriting in, 39–41
how to locate, 23–35, *34*
indexes of, 26–27
microfilmed, 27, 39
original, 37–39, 41–43
requesting copies of, 24, 34
published, 27
rules of conduct, 48–49
transcripts, using, 43–44
what to look for in, 39–42
*See also under individual
denominations*
city directories, 19–21, *20*
*Clerical Directory of the Protestant
Episcopal Church in the United
States of America, The*, 61

Coetus, German Reformed, 84
Colgate Library, 66
Columbia Theological Seminary,
125
Community of Christ, 92, 95–96
Deceased Members Card File
(1877–1995), 96
Library and Archives, 95–96
membership records, 95–96
Concordia Historical Institute, 100,
101
confirmation records. *See under
individual denominations*
Congregational Christian
Churches, 70, 85. *See also*
Congregational Church
Congregational Church, 69–73
administrative records, 72
ancestors, in registers of
Presbyterian churches, 69
baptism records, 6, *70*, 71
birth records, 70
charitable organizations,
70
conference records, 72–73
Congregational Library, 27,
71, 72
Congregational yearbooks,
72–73
Connecticut State Library,
records in, 21
death records, 70
denominational tree, 70
donations for, 49
financial records, 72
historical background, 47,
69–70
histories, 47, 72
immigration and migration,
7, *7*
in colonial New England, 16,
69
marriage records, 70
membership records, 7, 42,
70–72
ministers' records, 72–73
minute books, 72
narratives, colonial-era
conversion, 72
"Religious Records of New
York," records in, 21
*See also* Presbyterian
Congregationalism, on the frontier,
69
Conservative Grace Brethren
Churches, International, 83
Continuing Presbyterian Church,
125. *See also* Presbyterian
correspondence, in church papers,
50
county histories, 18
Cumberland Presbyterian Church,
124, 125. *See also* Presbyterian
*Cyclopedic Manual of the United*

*Presbyterian Church of North
America*, 126
Cyndi's List, Mennonite research
page, 106

# D

Danish
Baptist congregation minutes,
65
Latter-day Saint, 94
Lutheran, 98
Moravian, 88
Daughters of Utah Pioneers, 95
David Rumsey Historical Map
Collection, 19
death records. *See under individual
denominations*
*Deciphering Handwriting in German
Documents*, 82
denominational tree, 34–35. *See also
under individual denominations*
*Der Presbyterianer*, 127
*Diary, The*, 104
Digital Public Library of America,
18
Diocese of Dallas, 132
Diocese of Fort Wayne and South
Bend, Indiana, 131
Diocese of Gary, Indiana, 131
*Diocese of Northern Indiana Journal
of the Annual Council*, 61
Dioceses, Anglican, 60. *See also*
Anglican
directories, city, 19–21, *20*
*Directory of Maryland Church
Records*, 26
Disciples of Christ, 70
dismission, 8
*Doctrines and Discipline of the
Methodist Episcopal Church*, 110
donations, to church, 49
Dunkards. *See* Brethren, Church of
the Brethren
Dutch immigration and migration,
75–76, 77, 88, 94, 97
Dutch Reformed Church, 75–79
archives, 77
baptism records, 76
birth records, 77
church affiliation, 3
consistory minutes, 76–77
death records, 76, 77, 79
historical background, 75–76
immigration and migration, 16
in New York, 75
letter of transfer, *9*
marriage records, 6, 76, 77, 79
membership records, 76–78
ministers' records, 78
newspapers, 47, 78, 79
published indexes and
transcriptions, 78
records on Ancestry website,
26, 77

CPSIA information can be obtained
at www.ICGtesting.com
Printed in the USA
FSHW011206040819
60691FS